Every Session Counts

John Preston Nicolette Varzos Douglas Liebert

Every Session Counts

making the most
of your
brief therapy

Foreword by Simon Budman, Ph.D.

Impact Publishers®
San Luis Obispo, California 93406

Impact Publishers and colophon are registered trademarks of
Impact Publishers, Inc.

Library of Congress Cataloging-in-Publication Data

Preston, John,   1950-
    Every session counts : making the most of your brief therapy /
John Preston, Nicolette Varzos, Douglas Liebert.
        p.   cm.
    ISBN 0-915166-88-7 (pbk. : trade)
    1. Brief psychotherapy—Popular works.   2. Consumer education.
I. Varzos, Nicolette. II. Liebert, Douglas. III. Title.
RC480.55.P73   1995
616.89'14—dc20
                                                                          95-22724
                                                                          CIP

Cover design by Sharon Schnare, San Luis Obispo, California
Printed in the United States of America on acid-free paper

Published by **Impact ⧓ Publishers®**
POST OFFICE BOX 1094
SAN LUIS OBISPO, CALIFORNIA 93406

Dedications

To Arthur and Patty Browne, old friends, good friends.
— J.P.

For my children, Tanisha and Aaron.
— N.V.

*To my wife and children for what they've taught me, and their
love and support.*
— D.L.

Contents

Foreword

To the client and potential client —

Throughout healthcare there is an increasing emphasis on the patient/client as consumer. You are not just someone who comes in to see a therapist for treatment and passively has psychotherapy done to you. You have rights and responsibilities. There are ways that you can impact the course of your own therapy. I think that the best consumer is an informed consumer. I think that the best client for time-effective and brief therapy is one who is willing to fully participate as a partner in the treatment process. This book will help you in several ways. It will help you know what you are looking for from your therapy and therapist; it will also help you see how to take a full role in your own improvement.

You can ask questions, change the focus of treatment, suggest certain things to your therapist about your situation that he or she may not have thought about and so on. You can and should be a full partner in your treatment. *Every Session Counts* can help you do so.

To the therapist —

The thing I like most about this book is that it is practical. Preston, Varzos and Liebert obviously set out to write a volume that clients and potential clients could use and that therapists could recommend. They have clearly succeeded.

I have thought about the need for a book like this many times in the past. I always look for books I can suggest to the individuals and couples I see. How to keep the therapy alive between visits is a constant question for me. How to implement Milton Erickson's sage post-hypnotic suggestion, "My voice will go with you."

If you are trying to do brief or time-effective therapy in the current healthcare environment, you need as many tools as possible. It is becoming increasingly important to find ways to help the people we see actively be engaged in the therapeutic process *outside* of the confines of the office. This has always been the case, but we had the luxury not to think too much about it. When insurance benefits covered weekly, or multiple times per week treatment, if you didn't deal with an issue or the client made no progress in today's visit, maybe something would transpire in the next visit or the one after that. Few therapists can think like this anymore.

How can we, as clinicians, make every session count? In several ways: (1) *a well prepared* client is a client who can make the most of each visit; (2) through the use of *tasks and homework* assignments that carry the session into the "real world"; (3) by being *informed* about and *skilled* in methods of brief and time-effective therapy that have demonstrated value. I think that this book will help you help your clients more effectively. It will also help them be better informed participants in the therapy process.

— Simon H. Budman, Ph.D.
Newton, Massachusetts
July 16, 1995

Acknowledgements

Psychotherapy was born in the early part of the 20th century. Forms of treatment were created to help people face and survive the difficulties of life with less emotional strife. Yet until recently, most psychotherapies required a good deal of time and money. Such treatments were simply out of the reach of many ordinary folks.

The names David Malan, James Mann, Gregory Bateson, Peter Sifneos, Habib Davanlo, Aaron Beck, Simon Budman and Alan Gurman may not ring bells for those readers outside the field of psychology. But these innovative therapists have, during the past twenty-five years, pioneered approaches to emotional healing now simply referred to as "Brief Therapy." Their efforts have been directed toward the development of new and more effective approaches designed to reduce human emotional suffering in a much shorter period of time. We wish to acknowledge and honor these men and their work.

Many thanks to our superb editor, Dr. Robert Alberti, to the crew at Impact Publishers, and to Gail Lesh Johnson for her help with the preparation of the manuscript.

Finally, heartfelt thanks to our patients, our students, and our teachers. The most important lessons we have learned regarding emotional healing have come from you.

We sincerely hope this book will be of help to you or to someone you love who is going through difficult times.

Best wishes,

— John Preston, Nikki Varzos and Doug Liebert, 1995

1: Thinking About Getting Some Help?

"I've had this job for thirty years. I was at the top of my career. Then this young kid, straight out of school, with his fancy MBA comes in and pushes me out! What the hell am I supposed to do now? I've got bills to pay, kids, and now even my retirement is in question. How am I going to look in the job market now?! I feel so worthless. Nothing is right. I'm yelling at my wife for no reason and I feel terrible all the time."

Life really hits below the belt sometimes...
- Your employer just announced a 30% lay off.
- A loved one is killed in an accident.
- A child is diagnosed with a life-threatening illness.
- You can't keep up financially.
- A relationship is filled with anger and conflict.
- The demands of everyday living are weighing you down: picking up after the kids, cleaning the bathroom, paying bills.

Why does it seem we have to keep running harder than ever just to stay in the same place? Why is life sometimes so hard? Is it bad luck, or fate, or God's will, or carelessness, or the economy, or the government, or what?

One thing we all share in common is that sometimes we hurt. If you're reading this book, chances are you're looking for a way to stop hurting. You're used to solving your own problems, but this time you just can't seem to get a handle on it.

So you're thinking about getting some help. But the idea of therapy itself may be kind of scary. Will it help? How much will it cost? Will health insurance cover it? How do you find a therapist? Do you really want to tell a perfect stranger what's bothering you? Why can't you just solve your own problems?

In this book we'll help you answer those questions. We're going to tell you how *brief therapy* may help, what to expect if you seek therapy, and how you can help yourself improve your life.

As you grow older it seems that life challenges are on the increase and staying on top of them demands enormous effort. Think about it. Is there really anyone you know who hasn't been hit with some difficult life stresses? Problems add up, they hurt, and sometimes even overwhelm us.

There are times when you may need help to deal with the hurt; when life gets to be too much; when you feel you're coming apart at the seams.

Guilty, sad, anxious, overburdened, depressed — have you ever felt like that? Who hasn't? Always able to cope successfully before, this time you need a little help — from more than just your friends.

Do you have to be crazy to need help? No, just human. Like this distraught parent:

> *"I just read my kid's diary. She's doing LSD, crank and marijuana. I had no idea! She's just been suspended from school and wants to move out. What is she talking about, she's only 15 years old?! She stole my husband's car last night, was in a car accident, and they say it's her fault. Now what do we do?! I feel so helpless!"*

Even someone who has always been able to cope well, adapt to changing situations, and survive can be overcome by a sense of helplessness and loss. It can happen to any one of us at any time. And it can make us feel guilty, powerless, victimized, and overwhelmed.

There are times when you may need help to deal with the hurt: when life gets to be too much; when you feel you're coming apart at the seams. You don't have to be crazy to feel like that. All you have to be is human to know that living can be hard.

But Therapy? Isn't That for "Mental Illness"?

Not long ago, the idea of being "crazy" or "in therapy" brought to mind images of dark hospital corridors, locked rooms, a couch, and years of treatment from a "DOCTOR" who interpreted your every word while you spilled your guts. Most of us don't have first-hand experience with psychiatric treatment, but we can readily recall motion picture or television versions. (Let's face it, graphic and sensational images sell lots of TV advertising.) As a result, lots of folks figure that if you think you need therapy you must be *really* sick.

As a culture, we've generally valued self-sufficiency, and many people have mistakenly believed that those who suffer from emotional pain are either "stupid," "bad," "weak," or "nuts." To admit that you hurt like hell can add feelings of inadequacy or shame to your pain. And, if you have the idea that therapy is only for the "seriously mentally ill," you may just have kept it private and continued to suffer in silence.

The fact is that suffering is not rare and you're not alone. You hurt and are looking for something to take away the pain. Fortunately, help is available.

Lots of people go to counselors and therapists these days. From time to time everyone feels painful disappointments, losses, and conflicts with others. What you're feeling is a common and shared human experience. And you can get help. Not the type of help that lasts 25 years and costs hundreds of thousands of dollars. But effective, time-limited treatment — *brief therapy* — that can help you to resolve a crisis or painful situation, often in just a few sessions.

How Can a Few Sessions Really Help?

In brief therapy *every session counts*. It's not a fad, but a form of treatment developed and refined over many years that integrates effective procedures from a number of viewpoints. And it appears on the scene just in time, since most health insurance programs now cover only limited treatment.

Brief therapy can be as effective as long-term treatment for some people and some situations. This book will help you to understand a little more about brief therapy and what that choice and opportunity may mean to you.

To prepare yourself for your journey, here are a few keys to making brief therapy work for you:

1. *Determine if brief therapy is right for you* by learning what kind of problems respond best to brief treatment.

2. *Learn how you can make the most out of a few therapy sessions* by being an active participant, not a "couch potato."

3. *Learn what to expect* from brief therapy, what it can or cannot do for you, realistically.

4. *Learn to develop effective skills for coping* with the inevitable stresses of life, and thus help yourself reduce your stress and feel more in control of your life.

5. *Recognize that you may want treatment again,* at different times in your life, as new challenges appear. Brief Therapy focuses on your *current* problems — you can choose to come back if you need help in the future.

Remember, it's your life. You hold the key and the choice is yours. By seeking therapy, you are choosing to take responsibility for your life; to recognize and acknowledge your pain and humanness, and to find new strength within yourself. To help with this process, we'll be exploring what you can do to better problem-solve and cope in Part III of this book, "A Coping Skills Manual." We'll also explore the role of medications, and let you know how to use your community mental health service, university counseling center, or managed health care plan most effectively and efficiently.

Let's get started.

PART I
What Is Brief Therapy?

2: Is Brief Better?

When you're really sick, you probably make an appointment with your physician. The physician examines you, prescribes medicine, and — with time and good fortune — you're well again.

Psychotherapy began with a similar model: the "powerful doctor" healed the "sick patient." The patient may not have chosen to see a therapist, but was too ill to resist. It was generally assumed that a mentally ill patient would need treatment for a long time, if not forever. The relationship between the therapist and the patient reflected an unequal division of power, with the patient holding the short straw. Those earlier patients saw a therapist because they were "sick," not because of the problems of daily living.

Today people often make the choice to see a professional therapist — counselor, clinical social worker, marriage and family therapist, psychologist, or psychiatrist — when life feels too hard to deal with alone.

Today's clients know they won't be there for 20 years or have to recount every detail of childhood. This is not to say that long-term therapy doesn't have its place — brief therapy is not for everyone, nor is it appropriate for every problem (more on this in Chapter Seven) — but for many people, a brief intervention can offer much needed help, support, and emotional relief.

Hire a Consultant!

If your finances are complex, or if you're having financial problems, you might decide to hire an accountant. The accountant would assist you in some creative problem-solving, show you how you could work out your difficulties with income, expenses and taxes, and ultimately help you to make the best choices.

Similarly, if you were physically out of shape and decided to get healthy, you might go to a gym and hire a fitness instructor. A fitness professional would assess your condition, guide you through exercises appropriate to your current abilities and physical state, and help you choose exercises suited to your particular needs and goals.

When living gets hard, you could go shopping (some folks call this "retail therapy"). You may find temporary relief — or escape — this way. But you'll probably spend less and enjoy it more in the long run if you hire a *mental health consultant.*

Is your mental health as important to you as your physical well-being? You don't stay in shape by being lucky, you have to work at it. A strong marriage is the result of hard work. And a healthy mind and attitude may at times require a little outside help and maintenance — a kind of "tune-up" for how you think and feel.

When you view a therapist as your mental health consultant, the unequal division of power seen in earlier years is gone. You alone made the decision to enter therapy — no one made that decision for you. You may be in pain and seeking relief, but that doesn't mean that you can't be an educated and informed consumer.

The best, most effective way to feel better is to become an active and knowledgeable participant in your treatment process.

Your mental health consultant is there for you as a facilitator of change, healing, and growth. Like the fitness consultant who doesn't "cure" but rather provides direction, guidance, and support, the mental health consultant is an agent of change working with you, to help you through the difficult times. A therapist can, for example, help you to learn more effective problem-solving skills, resulting in greater self-confidence and increased ability to cope with your current problems.

Maybe you'd prefer to be your own mental health consultant? Here are a couple of things to keep in mind: emotional pain is considerably more intense when it is experienced alone; and none of us can be completely objective about our own circumstances.

Your mental health consultant won't and can't do the work for you, but will listen objectively and help guide you toward the results that *you* choose. In brief therapy, attention is focussed on here-and-now issues. Each life experience gives you and your consultant the chance to examine your thoughts, beliefs, perceptions, and attitudes and how they work for and against you in your daily living.

Your therapist isn't there to "fix" or "change" you, but to build on your strengths. The consultant is your guide to understanding the complex nature of stressful events and how they are related to your thoughts, attitudes, and beliefs about yourself and your world.

A therapist/consultant can help you reduce your pain, minimize future disasters, and develop action plans and strategies for growth and healing now and in the future. The emphasis in brief therapy is not on "sick patients" and "powerful doctors." It's on people in distress making wise choices so they can take charge of their lives.

Why Brief Therapy?

Since psychotherapy arrived on the scene in the early part of the 20th century, this form of treatment has been considered to be a lengthy endeavor. Especially those therapists advocating traditional Freudian analysis insisted that for therapy to be beneficial, it had to be intense and long-term. So those few who were able to afford it entered analysis and visited their therapist *three to five times a week for many months, and often many years.* Psychoanalysis was often helpful for the very small group of therapy clients who could afford it. And, because it was the treatment of choice for the "rich and famous," it became the approach glorified by the media — and therefore desired by the rest of the population.

What's wrong with this picture? First, long-term psychotherapy is extremely expensive and thus is far out of the reach of most people. Human emotional suffering is widespread and affects people from all walks of life, rich and poor alike. Second, extensive psychological research finds little compelling scientific evidence that, overall, long-term psychotherapy is more effective than brief therapy. In fact, the majority of people looking for therapy prefer short-term psychotherapy and greatly benefit much from the experience.

What is "Brief Therapy"?

Generally brief therapy is defined as psychotherapy lasting from one to twenty sessions. In the contemporary "managed care" environment, and in most public treatment settings (community mental health, university counseling centers), brief therapy averages between three and ten sessions

In the United States more than 8 million people see a therapist each year and 85% of them are treated with brief therapy.

This shorter course of treatment — fewer sessions and thus significantly lower costs — makes psychotherapy available to *many* more people.

Sometimes therapy must be brief because insurance companies, mental health clinics, counseling centers and HMO's have limits on the mental health benefits that they offer. However, shorter-term psychotherapy is often brief by design. Short-term therapy includes special techniques that can speed up the process, and the results are often better than for long-term therapy.

Brief therapy, however, is not only defined by the length of treatment. There are a number of goals and characteristics of brief therapy that set it apart from longer forms of psychological treatment. The key elements include:

- Focus on a *specific problem,* not on "reshaping your personality."
- *Active involvement* of both client and therapist.
- Emphasis on *solutions* to life problems, not causes.
- *Time-limited* course of treatment.

We'll take a look at how it works in the next chapter.

3: Off the Couch and Into Action

Most brief therapy approaches are "action oriented." Every session really does count. With only a few sessions available, clients cannot afford to be passive or to gradually explore their concerns, feelings, past and present experiences. The process requires rapid identification of and attention to the primary area of greatest current concern. Therapists call this establishing a *focus*.

It's not that other issues or life experiences are unimportant. Rather, in brief therapy, you and your therapist together will identify and agree to work on *the* most important or urgent concern in your life right now (this may be, for example, a particular symptom, such as depression or panic attacks, or a particular life struggle, such as resolving conflicts with an employer, or learning more effective ways to resolve marital problems). Once you and your therapist have clearly identified "the problem," this focus becomes the central issue to be discussed in therapy sessions.

• A second way that brief therapy is "active," is that the therapist is more likely to speak out in therapy sessions. In contrast to some forms of therapy where the therapist stays pretty quiet, in brief therapy there generally are more questions, answers, feedback and active problem solving.

• A third way that brief therapy is lively is that it really encourages the client to *take action*. This may be in the form of between-sessions *homework assignments* (e.g., keeping a personal journal; monitoring progress by the use of self-rating check lists; trying out new behaviors in life situations). We'll talk more about this later in the book. Thus, a lot goes on outside the therapy room and between sessions. Many clients enjoy these activities that make them more active participants in their treatment, feeling that they are better able to "take charge."

• One more way that brief therapy is action-oriented is through developing the client's "tool kit" for dealing with stressful situations, including life skills for: *Interpersonal coping:* more effective and practical ways to problem-solve and resolve conflicts with friends, relatives, coworkers, and important others; and *Internal stress reduction:* powerful ways to reduce anxiety, sadness, despair, and irritability.

One important benefit of increasing your coping skills is that you may discover these skills offer you a much greater sense of control and mastery in everyday life situations, reducing feelings of helplessness and powerlessness. Coping skills may be taught in individual or group therapy sessions, or with the use of self-help books. Part Three of this book provides a brief coping skills manual that describes a number of effective approaches. You may find this very helpful as you are going though your brief therapy experience.

Living one's life, meeting challenges, surviving hard times and growing are life-long processes.

Brief therapy can best be seen as an important experience or tool that helps people as they hit those inevitable hard times throughout life. The goal of brief therapy is not to "cure," but to provide support, to facilitate growth, and to increase effective coping.

> *No one ever gets completely "cured," totally emotionally healthy, or immune to the pain of human experiences of loss, disappointment or frustration.*

Research shows that people can change and experience benefits while *in* brief therapy, but it doesn't end there. A good deal of growth and "work" continues after therapy has ended. The last session of brief therapy, in a very real sense, is not *the end*. After the final session, clients put newly learned skills into action, acting as their own "therapists." Following a course of brief therapy, one of the authors received a note from a woman client stating:

> *"I stopped coming to therapy sessions three months ago, but it's like I'm still in treatment. I often hear your voice in my mind saying 'Remember to be decent to yourself' or 'It's okay to give*

yourself permission to be who you are and to feel what you feel'...I also kinda do therapy with myself...and it helps a lot."

The time spent in therapy may be "brief," but life doesn't stop handing us challenges, frustrations, joys and hopes. No one ever stops growing; no one ever has it all figured out.

It is not uncommon for clients to go through two or more courses of brief therapy, at various times in life. At 24, Sara saw a therapist seven times for help as her marriage floundered and she and her husband became more distant with each other. She also attended a group for couples. The therapy and support group helped Sara and Ken to find new ways of balancing their relationship, and they stayed together. Nine years later, following the death of her mother, Sara returned to her therapist to help her deal with her loss. They met for six sessions, though her grieving continued well past the time of her last session. However, therapy had helped her to accept the reality of her mom's death and the depth of her sorrow. She began to feel more "ok" about expressing her sadness to her husband and her kids. She was clearly on the road to emotional healing from this painful life event.

No therapy is a magical solution or a cure-all for the painful things that happen to us as human beings. Brief therapy can, however, be a tremendously important resource during painful times, and a foundation for successfully handling the tough times that may come later.

4: What's Therapy Like?

It's not what you think.

You've had glimpses of psychotherapy in books, in the movies and on television. Forget them. It's not likely that what you've seen has prepared you for what really goes on.

If you're like most folks, you're thinking about therapy because you're experiencing significant pain — perhaps desperation — in your life. (Almost no one goes to therapy for the small stuff.) Under such times of great stress and personal uncertainty, everyone wants and needs to feel safe, and to feel some assurance that the decision to see a therapist was the right one.

Most folks have lots of questions about this business of telling one's troubles to a total stranger:

"What actually happens in therapy?"
"What can I expect to get from therapy?"
"What are reasonable and attainable benefits I might gain from therapy?"
"Is there a reasonable chance of getting the help I need?"
"Will it be worth the time, money, effort and emotional distress to become involved in a course of brief therapy?"

Good questions! In this chapter and the two that follow, we are going to offer you some straight talk about psychotherapy, and present how some people really benefit from their experience of brief therapy. As we address your expectations of brief therapy, we'll focus on three topics: what's expected of you, what actually happens during therapy sessions; and, in the next chapter, what therapists are really like.

What's Expected of You

• You may be asked to fill out a background questionnaire to help the therapist determine if treatment with you is appropriate, and as a means of learning about details of your history (e.g., educational history, number of people in your family, prior psychotherapy experiences, medical history...).

• To do your best to share openly your particular concerns, thoughts and feelings.

• To complete assigned and agreed tasks — homework assignments — outside the therapy hour. (More about this in Chapter 16.)

• To show up for sessions as scheduled and to pay agreed-upon professional fees. To give advance notice in case of a cancellation (except in cases of last-minute emergencies).

• You may be asked to complete one or more psychological tests to help your therapist assess your personal situation and needs.

What Actually Happens During Therapy Sessions?

Therapy sessions vary a lot, depending on who you are, what current problems you're experiencing and the kind of therapist you hire. We can, however, give you a summary glimpse of the "typical" course of brief therapy.

PHASE ONE: *Getting Acquainted and Discussing What Concerns You Most*. Effective therapists help the therapy process to get under way, often by asking their clients, "What are the main reasons you've decided to come to therapy?" or, "I'd like to know what's most on your mind and what you'd like to accomplish in coming to therapy." The early sessions generally are designed to help you feel more at ease and to begin discussing your main problems or concerns. At this beginning phase, many people entering therapy are unclear about how they are feeling, *or* they may be self-critical, for example, "I shouldn't be feeling this way." You and your therapist will be forming a "therapeutic alliance" — a working partnership which will help you get past your uncertainty and reach your goals in therapy.

PHASE TWO: *Finding a Focus*. As the discussion continues in further sessions, your therapist will do a lot of listening and ask lots of questions to help you pinpoint a major *focus* — the major issue or problem you'll be dealing with in therapy. You and your therapist will identify specific problems, and find out in what ways these issues are especially important to you at this time in your life.

Psychotherapy (brief or long-term) doesn't provide a quick fix, of course. In fact, people may find that they feel worse during the first couple of sessions of therapy — at least more keenly aware of distressing feelings. And the reality often is that once a person begins to take a close look at difficult issues, emotional pain may be felt more intensely. If this happens to you, *don't bail out!* It's natural, normal and fairly predictable — but an essential part of coming to terms with life issues that hurt. Fortunately for most, emotional distress at some point subsides as they begin to get a handle on life problems and cope more effectively.

PHASE THREE: *Refocusing or Tuning Into the Problem.* A common experience during the third phase of brief therapy is for clients to begin to understand their problems, and themselves, in a new light. Many times this involves a change of perspective and attitude. Such "problems" as being oversensitive to criticism, feeling taken advantage of by others, missing a loved one who has died, feeling overwhelmed and frustrated at work, start to seem more "understandable." The problems may seem just as painful, undesirable or frustrating — however, many folks start to think "My feelings make sense to me now," or "Of course I feel this way." The volume gets turned down on harsh self-criticism.

Attitudes Can Shift During Therapy

From	To
This is crazy.	I don't like the way this feels.
I shouldn't be so upset.	I'm upset. What can I do about it?
This shouldn't be happening!	I don't want this to happen, but it is and it's upsetting.
I'm confused. What the hell is the matter with me?	Of course I feel this way!

PHASE FOUR: Action-Oriented Skills...Practice, Practice, Practice. "Now I know more clearly what I feel and I don't condemn myself so harshly. But I still feel bad. What do I do next?"

Often in brief therapy, once the major problems or concerns have been clarified, the focus is shifted toward active problem-solving. Kimberly, for example, learned ways to reduce anxiety by providing more inner support for herself prior to taking an exam at school. Roberto developed more assertive ways to communicate his feelings and needs to his wife. In one of his therapy sessions, Doug carefully planned out just how he was going to approach his shop foreman to share concerns he had about the work environment. Sherri began to write in her personal journal, discovered more about her own feelings, and learned to give herself permission to grieve the loss of her brother.

Brief therapy became a place for these people to think things through, come to conclusions regarding actions they wanted to take, learn some new coping skills and practice these skills during the session. As Roberto said, "Having a therapist is kinda like having a coach. You can plan out what you want to do, practice it, get some feedback, refine it, and then get the extra shove you need to do it for real in your life."

PHASE FIVE: Fine Tuning. In the final stages of brief therapy, often people find it helpful to summarize what's happened. It helps to be clear about several points:

- This was my problem
- I came to see it as understandable...not "crazy"
- I felt more okay about wanting to make a change
- I figured out which approaches work for me and which don't
- I felt supported by my therapist
- I put coping skills into action
- I got some results

Getting better and feeling better usually aren't just due to fate or good luck. You have to work at changing and discovering what helps.

Once you know how to cope more successfully, you're better prepared for the next time life becomes difficult.

Of course, it's not all this simple! And experiences vary a lot. But the phases we've talked about here describe a pretty common experience in brief therapy. Most people who succeed in therapy don't feel ultimately "cured" or "fixed," but they do feel better. They leave therapy knowing that they've done some real *work,* and it was *their effort* that paid off. In particular, the most common outcome of successful brief therapy is feeling more okay about who you are!

Some of the specific results you may realistically expect from brief therapy are discussed in Chapter 6. First, however, let's take a look at this person called "therapist."

5: What Are Therapists Like?

T herapists are human beings.

"Obviously," you may say. Perhaps, but some folks seem to think that therapy is a magical art, practiced by individuals with x-ray vision and wise advice for every life problem. The fact is that therapists are highly trained experts in human behavior who are just as vulnerable as the rest of the population to all of the realities of being human.

In this chapter, we'll review the characteristics that allow competent professional therapists to offer that special "helping relationship" that assists people in making sense of their lives during emotionally stressful times.

What Makes Therapists Different?
• *Therapists generally don't give advice.* Many folks probably can benefit from helpful suggestions and good advice from time to

time, but such input is readily available from friends and relatives (sometimes even when you don't want it). Truth to tell, most therapists aren't really any better at giving common sense advice than anyone else. But they can and do provide a kind of help not readily found in one's ordinary network of family and friends.

• *Therapists are trained to understand emotional distress and the process of emotional recovery.* In a sense they are people who understand the general terrain of the human landscape, and can help guide people through painful times towards growth and healing.

• *Therapists are willing and able to face very strong emotions.* It's hard to really be with someone when they are experiencing intense feelings. To have to witness human suffering in itself is difficult. It is also hard for many people to experience another's pain without it touching on their own inner feelings. Good therapists have learned to handle these issues, to be fully

> *Good therapists have learned to be fully present with their patients... to transmit an attitude of respect, understanding, and acceptance.*

present with their psychotherapy clients, to resonate with their pain, but to also maintain an appropriate objectivity. Thus a client is able to express strong feelings and know that the therapist cares, yet is not overwhelmed or blown-away by the powerful emotions. This provides a considerable amount of stability and safety within the therapy hour.

• *Good therapists tend to be non-judgemental.* They understand that most interpersonal and emotional problems can be seen as attempts to emotionally survive the common problems in living. Effective therapists transmit an attitude of respect, understanding, and acceptance. In psychotherapy outcome studies, the most commonly reported factor judged to have been helpful by therapy clients was the therapist's ability to genuinely care and to understand the client. The therapist's compassionate attitude helps the client to reduce excessive self-criticism and develop an enhanced capacity for self-acceptance.

- *Therapists provide support for self-expression.* This kind of support and encouragement of honest expression helps shore-up and solidify the development of the self. To use an analogy, when building a concrete wall, boards are used to provide support for the concrete as it begins to harden. At some point the boards can be removed and the wall is solid; the concrete has developed its own strength and it can stand on its own. In therapy, it begins to feel okay to talk openly about how things really are. Although reduction of emotional distress (e.g.,. decreased depression, anxiety, tension, etc.) is a primary goal for most people entering treatment, one of the most common results of psychotherapy is an increased sense of self and self-esteem. "When my therapist really listens, I know it's okay to be me!"

- *Therapists help clients to maintain a sense of realistic hope during difficult times.* Not phony, "Everything will be all right" hope, but rather a realistic perspective and a trust in the process that working through and psychotherapy will very likely lead to healing.

- *Therapists do not repeat maladaptive patterns of interaction.* Many relationships involve patterns. A very dependent, seemingly helpless person may frequently enter into relationships where her behavior leads others to treat her like a child. This repetitive "interpersonal dance" may feel good at first (because it is familiar), but ultimately contributes to keeping her stuck; she never grows up. The tendency for others to rush in and rescue this "helpless" person keeps her stuck in an infantile position. A good therapist would empathize with her distress, but would resist the urge to treat her like a helpless child. The therapist's refusal to perpetuate the dance allows this woman to grow and come to feel her own strength.

What You Can Expect from the Therapist

All competent psychotherapists are committed to a code of ethics and a standard of practice that attempts to assure the following (essential ingredients in a helping relationship):

- To provide privacy and confidentiality.[1]

---

[1] In most states laws regarding confidentiality are limited i.e., there are certain instances when confidentiality does not apply. See Appendix A for specifics on confidentiality.

- To treat clients in a decent and respectful manner.
- To gain the client's informed consent for any procedures undertaken in the course of therapy.
- To provide realistic emotional support.
- To help you feel more at ease during the first meetings. Many people are worried about the first session; "I won't know what to say or where to start"..."I feel anxious about talking to someone I don't know." These concerns are common and very understandable; it's normal to feel nervous during the first sessions. Effective therapists know how to help people get started talking.
- To be "neutral" — non-critical and non-judgemental. An important goal in therapy is not to judge people, but rather to understand and be helpful.
- To be honest. Your therapist is there to help you more fully understand yourself, your patterns of behavior, your feelings. You'll get some honest and objective feedback about your attitudes and actions. The feedback will feel good when it recognizes your strengths, and it may feel uncomfortable when it points out your weaknesses. Brief therapy can help you capitalize on your strengths and transform your weaknesses into strengths. The process may be uncomfortable at times, but the outcome may be even more positive than you expect.
- To make sure that the relationship is strictly professional. This is what psychotherapists refer to as "maintaining appropriate professional boundaries." It is a part of the therapists' ethical code to assure that therapy remains safe. In the practice of psychotherapy, relating to a patient in other-than-professional ways — socially, romantically, in business deals — is generally inappropriate, and may be unethical or even illegal. Sexually intimate relationships are absolutely prohibited by the professional codes of ethics (and the law in most states). Social friendships outside the therapy hour and business deals are unwise, and may also be unethical.
- To make appropriate referrals. Sometimes your therapist may need to refer you to a medical doctor, to make a referral for psychiatric

evaluation and possible medication treatment, to refer to another mental health therapist who offers particular services (e.g., marital counseling), to refer to support groups/programs when appropriate (e.g., Alcoholics Anonymous, bereavement support groups, etc.). Your therapist may even refer you to another therapist if both of you feel that the current therapy isn't working.

• To provide information about the therapist's education and training, fees, types of services offered, and responses to any number of other relevant questions regarding the treatment he/she provides.

Types of Mental Health Therapists

Psychiatrists (M.D.): Psychiatrists are medical doctors who have received specialized training in the treatment of emotional problems, including both medication and psychological treatments. (It is possible for a physician to practice psychiatry without specialized training, however very few do so.) Most psychiatrists treat emotional disorders with medications. Some psychiatrists also provide psychotherapy, behavior therapy, or cognitive therapy.

Psychologists: Almost all hold a doctorate degree in psychology (Ph.D., Psy.D., Ed.D.), have a number of years postgraduate training in psychological methods, and in most states are licensed or certified to practice. They also have specialized training in the administration and interpretation of psychological tests.

Clinical Social Workers: Generally hold a masters degree (M.S.W.), have considerable supervised experience and are usually licensed by the state (hence the designation, "L.C.S.W." - Licensed Clinical Social Worker).

Marriage Family and Child Counselors/Therapists: A number of states grant a license or certificate to Marriage, Family and Child Counselors (or Marriage, Family and Child Therapists). Such therapists generally have at least a masters degree in counseling (M.A. or M.S.), usually with specialization in treatment of marriage and family problems or problems of children and adolescents.

Pastoral Counselors: Some clergy have received training in counseling and may provide supportive therapy to members of their church or to others desiring a therapist who addresses both emotional and spiritual concerns.

Getting the Most from Your Therapist

• *The chemistry has to be "good enough."* You need to feel a degree of comfort and compatibility with your therapist. Not all people are going to make a good connection with even very good therapists. It may not be essential to feel 100% comfortable with your therapist, but it is quite important to feel the following: a basic sense of trust, the perception that you and your feelings are being treated with respect, and some degree of confidence that your therapist is competent. First and foremost good therapists, beyond being well-trained and skilled, need to be basically good, decent people.

• *The type of treatment must be appropriate:* Not all problems are best approached in the same manner. A good therapist will evaluate your situation and within the first session or two talk with you about what kind of treatment he/she recommends. Some types of emotional problems are due either in part or in full to medical/biochemical disturbances. Medical treatment and/or psychiatric medication treatment may be helpful or even necessary (see Chapter 18).

• *The treatment must do no harm:* Any approach that is powerful enough to help can be powerful enough to cause harm, if in the hands of an incompetent or destructive therapist. Most licensed therapists are well trained and are helpful to most of their clients. However, as in any other profession, incompetence and/or unethical behavior does exist. *You are entitled to competent and ethical treatment.* Anything else should be reported to appropriate institutional or regulatory agencies.

6: Realistic Results

"**F**rom miserable to marvelous!"

So boasted a recent ad for a psychotherapist in the *Yellow Pages*. Such promises of miraculous "transformation," in our opinion, are at best misguided, and at worst unethical, preying on the desperate needs of suffering and vulnerable people.

At the heart of any truly healing psychotherapy is a commitment to the truth. Well-trained therapists know the benefits of psychological treatment and the limitations. In all honesty, there is no way to ever know for sure ahead of time how much you may benefit from treatment. All that is really known is that effective treatments do exist and large-scale outcome studies have shown that the majority of clients can benefit from brief therapy. The fact also remains that some people do not benefit — and some (a small minority) get worse.

Many times psychotherapy is literally "life saving" (for example, in helping to prevent suicide). However, for most people brief therapy is likely to yield less dramatic positive benefits. As we examine some of the common outcomes from brief therapy in this chapter, remember that there is no guarantee that everyone will benefit. Nevertheless, these do represent realistic and rather typical results.

- *Feeling less depressed, anxious and tense.*[1]

- *Feeling better about who you are and your ability to manage your life.* This can take many forms. Before they enter therapy, many people erroneously conclude "I'm crazy...I'm neurotic...I'm weak and inadequate...or I'm screwed up." For many, many psychotherapy clients, an important experience in therapy is developing a new view

---

[1]Psychotherapy outcome research has shown that symptom reduction (specifically anxiety and depression) is one of the most significant and common results from brief therapy. Often short term treatment for anxiety and depression may involve both psychotherapy and psychiatric medication (see Chapter 18).

or belief about themselves. Very negative, self-critical views, like those noted above, usually give way to more compassionate, more realistic beliefs: "Of course I'm sad... this is what people feel when they've had a serious loss"... or, "I *am* sensitive to criticism and it irritates me when my wife is overly critical toward me"... or "I certainly don't like feeling so upset by this rejection, but I understand why it hurts so much. This relationship meant a lot to me!"

The change to such realistic views can lead to changes in how you feel about yourself. Therapy clients commonly adopt more realistic, healthy, and decent attitudes toward themselves.

- *"Getting clear."* Clients typically experience increased clarity about how they *really* feel about things, what they want and need, what they value, how they honestly see other people and what things in life really matter to them.

Among the myriad inner feelings, beliefs and thoughts you hold, many were taught you by your parents, teachers and other influential people during your early years. Such "implanted" beliefs and thoughts (what some psychologists call "injunctions") may be helpful and agree with your own more personal values: "I really am a good-hearted person" or "It's important to try my best at tasks that are challenging."

Unfortunately, implanted thoughts can also be more self-critical or negative: "You're just going to fail no matter what you do, so why try?" or "Real men don't cry, so if I cry, I should feel ashamed."

Have you heard — or told yourself — any of these?

Common Negative Injunctions

Don't be emotional.	Don't cry.
Don't rock the boat.	Don't get your hopes up.
Grow up! Don't be childish.	Don't ask for strokes.
Don't get too close.	Don't really trust people.
Don't trust your feelings, body, gut reactions.	Be logical.
	Don't get mad.
Don't do better than mom/dad.	Be perfect.
Try harder, stick with it, don't give up, don't let go.	Please others.
	Be strong.

As you begin in therapy to talk openly and honestly about feelings and thoughts, a common outcome is that you will, at some point, become more and more clear about which thoughts and beliefs arise from your inner, true self, and which thoughts or beliefs feel somewhat alien.

As you begin to talk openly and honestly about feelings and thoughts, you will become more clear about which thoughts and beliefs arise from your inner, true self, and which feel somewhat alien.

Getting clear about how you really and truly feel (believe, think, value...) can be important in two respects: *first,* you are then in a better position to make decisions or take actions that "feel right" based on your true inner beliefs. This may lead to greater ease in decision making and an increased sense of self-confidence, and, *second,* a very common consequence can be a more solid *sense of self.* This last experience is a bit hard to define, but is an important and common outcome. It is often described by people as feeling more "real," "alive," "authentic" or "whole," and feeling better able to hold on to your inner awareness of "what *I* truly want, desire, believe in, or need." (see Chapter 17).

• *Accepting yourself.* Stressful life events often make us feel anger, sadness or fear. And yet, for many of us, to actually admit these feelings to ourselves or to express such emotions leads to feelings of shame, self-criticism or anxiety. A very common outcome from brief therapy is a new sense of okay-ness about being "you," accepting who you are, and expressing it without shame or self-criticism.

• *Developing more effective problem-solving skills, ways of coping with stress, and new approaches to handling interpersonal problems.*

• *Learning important life lessons,* for example:

♦ I may have some short-comings, but I am what I am, and that's not so bad.

♦ Some emotional pain is inevitable and in the long run, probably necessary. You can't just grit your teeth and hope it will go away. Losses have to be mourned.

♦ In most instances, the expression of feelings is not dangerous (e.g., expressing anger or sadness).

♦ I have a right to be who I am... to be true to myself (my values, beliefs, my life style), even though some people may not agree nor be able to accept me.

♦ Life may seem unbearable during a tremendously painful situation, but you ultimately survive.

♦ It's easy to lose perspective when you are in the middle of stressful times; yet most of the time, even very difficult circumstances only last a while. With time, most people discover inner strengths and resources, and are able to get back on their feet and move ahead with their lives.

♦ Sometimes you have to modify your wishes and hopes, learn to endure frustration and accept "half a loaf."[1]

♦ Just wishing doesn't produce results. In order to reach goals, one needs to act, to take specific action steps.

♦ You can't always get what you want.

♦ Certain ways of thinking, acting and behaving, interpersonal behaviors and attitudes simply don't work and in the long run are self-defeating. In general, "cooperation" is a good technique for getting along with people.[1]

♦ If you take a good and honest look at your early life — the way you were treated, the general emotional atmosphere in your home — it will probably begin to make sense to you why certain things are especially emotionally painful (e.g., in a family atmosphere of extreme shaming and criticism, it is understandable that a person might grow up being especially sensitive to criticism).

♦ Ultimately you are responsible for your own actions.

♦ Honesty (generally) is the best policy.

You may never come to agree with all of these ideas, but we encourage you to work toward a positive view of your capacity to *direct your own life.* That, after all, may be the single most important lesson of all.

---

[1]Adapted from Strupp (1969)

7: When Brief Is Not Enough

Even though brief therapy can be very helpful for many people, it is not always the appropriate course of action.

Sometimes, brief psychotherapy is simply not enough. Some people have gone through tremendously difficult times and have very deep emotional wounds that require longer treatment. Their problems involve not just one major focus, but several. Serious difficulties may affect many aspects of life. Brief therapy can provide a starting point for such folks, and many are able to make some gains. But those who have a lot of healing or growth to do, while able to benefit from brief treatment, may subsequently enter either a support group or longer-term therapy.

For two types of emotional problems, brief therapy is probably not a good idea at all. Those who have experienced *extreme* psychological traumas in childhood (physical, emotional or sexual abuse, or severe neglect) find that the intensity and depth of their emotional pain may not be adequately addressed in brief therapy. For them, there is the risk that a little therapy may open up emotional flood gates, without the opportunity to truly resolve and work through the pain. In such cases, brief therapy can be worse than ineffective — it can be harmful.

People with severe, chronic mental illnesses (e.g., schizophrenia, manic-depressive or bi-polar illness, severe personality disorders) are not likely to benefit much from brief therapy. These major emotional disorders almost always require long-term supportive treatment and/or psychiatric medication.

Some symptoms always warrant a referral for intensive psychiatric treatment. Here's a brief summary of signs of serious psychiatric illness:

• Extreme confusion, erratic behavior, hallucinations and very unrealistic thoughts are signs of *Psychosis* (e.g., schizophrenia).

- Severe mood swings and manic episodes (times of very high energy, agitation, decreased need for sleep, rapid speech) may indicate *Bi-Polar (manic depressive) Disorder.*

- A history of intense, often chaotic relationships with others; intense, volatile emotions of jealousy, anger, hostility, loneliness; bouts of drug or alcohol abuse, multiple suicide attempts, and/or self-mutilation all may be signs of *severe personality disorders.*

- With significant alcohol or other substance abuse, brief therapy may be helpful, but only after successfully attaining sobriety. Such individuals *must* first seek treatment from a 12-step program such as Alcoholics Anonymous or a professional chemical dependency treatment program.

"...major emotional disorders almost always require long-term supportive treatment and/or psychiatric medication."

The bottom line: The conditions summarized above indicate a number of exceptions, but the vast majority of people seeking psychotherapy can and do benefit from brief approaches. Chances are you'll find it valuable if your own circumstances do not involve one of these more serious conditions.

Long-Term Psychotherapy: Another Formula for Healing and Growth

Some emotional difficulties clearly require intensive and lengthy psychological treatment. However, you don't need to be in serious emotional pain to benefit from long-term therapy. As we've seen, brief therapy can help most people deal with fairly specific life problems, but many folks have chosen longer-term treatment for resolution of psychological issues and personal growth. As we sing the praises of brief therapy, we certainly don't want to overlook or underrate the value of long-term psychotherapeutic treatment.

PART II
How Does Therapy Help?

Y̲ou'll get more benefit from therapy if you understand how the process works to help heal emotional difficulties. In the chapters that make up this part of the book, we have identified several key themes that describe the healing process in therapy. Our hope is that, by understanding more about how therapy works, you'll not only get more out of your therapy experience, but you'll also realize those gains more quickly.

As you'll learn in chapters 8-12, therapy can help you move:

From Distress to Healing
From Talk that Hurts to Talk that Helps
From Confusion to Clarity
From Illusion to Reality
From Isolation to Contact.

8: From Distress to Healing

S̲tress is a part of all our lives.

We all encounter ordinary daily stresses and, sooner or later, everyone will experience especially difficult (sometimes tragic) times. A degree of emotional suffering is unavoidable. This is just the truth... part of the price of membership in the human race.

Job stress, marital conflicts, on-going medical problems or chronic pain, financial worries, fears about the future, betrayal by a good friend, the list goes on. As we go through difficult times, we all have inner reactions. Whether or not our emotions are expressed outwardly has a lot to do with our culture and society, our upbringing (e.g., some people are raised to stifle emotions, grit their teeth, and be "tough"), and personality style (e.g., some folks are simply private people, who prefer to deal with emotions in an internal way, and aren't likely to share distressing feelings with others).

However, *major stressful events nearly always have an impact on people.* It is rare to simply feel no effect of major distressing events. If the event is devastating enough, some individuals will bury their emotional responses. Nevertheless, those responses almost always will find an outlet — somehow, sometime.

To successfully make it through hard times and to benefit from therapy, to a degree, you must face the reality of their pain (e.g.,sadness, frustration, anger, fear, loneliness...). At the same time, let's be clear: *there is nothing inherently noble about suffering great pain.* Some people say that it builds character or is some kind of test of strength or spiritual fiber. But the bottom line is that pain hurts, and it is very normal to want to reduce suffering.

Dealing with Emotional Pain: Mind... Body... Action!

There are three main paths we humans follow as we try to deal with emotional pain. Whether a conscious choice or an "automatic response," the key avenues are the mind, the body, and direct action:

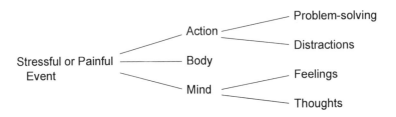

Action: Overt action generally has two aims: problem-solving or distraction. Problem-solving action may involve going directly to a person with whom there is a conflict, speaking with him or her, and asking for some kind of change in behavior or other resolution. Distracting actions, on the other hand, are usually taken to help one ignore or minimize emotional pains or distress. Examples of such actions include: workaholism; watching T.V.; engaging in sports; numbing oneself with alcohol, tranquilizers, and other drugs; overeating; taking the focus off yourself by picking a fight or arguing with others; or sexually acting-out. (A quick romantic involvement with a new person in the aftermath of a divorce may be a temporary distraction from inner feelings of sadness and loss.)

Body. Physical changes are a very natural part of emotional responses (e.g., increased blood pressure, insomnia, tension headaches, fatigue). When people go to great extremes to avoid feeling inner emotions and in essence, grit their teeth, a very common result is the emergence of stress-related physical symptoms. These symptoms can range from discomfort and annoyance, to life-threatening conditions (e.g., severe high blood pressure, heart attacks...).

Mind. The final major outlet for emotional pain is in the mind, experienced either as *feelings* or as *thoughts*. Those who notice mainly inner feelings may find that powerful emotions erupt: waves of sadness, panicky feelings, outbursts of anger. Those who are aware mainly or their inner thoughts typically experience continual fretting, recurrent painful memories, and/or worries about possible future calamities.

If your only way to deal with emotional pain is through distracting actions or by stressing your body, it's likely you won't fully heal from emotionally painful events — feelings of loss, sadness, hurt, despair — and that you'll continue to hurt on a deep inner level. If you're carrying a burden of unresolved distress, it's hard to truly heal your emotional problems.

Most therapists agree that our best shot at emotional healing and resolution lies in facing the reality of painful events, the truth of inner emotions, and processing the experiences through the mind (accessing inner feelings *and* thoughts). We'll explore more about how this is done shortly.

We've found it helpful to talk about two different kinds of emotional pain: "necessary pain" and "unnecessary pain." *Necessary emotional pain* is basic, common, honest human anguish virtually anyone would feel when they encounter a very tough life event, like the loss of a child, being fired, going through a divorce, major surgery. If you get burned, it hurts. You have little choice but to feel the pain. And, likewise, this is true with necessary *emotional* pain. Certain life events just hurt.

> *"Most therapists agree that our best shot at emotional healing lies in facing the reality of painful events and processing the experiences..."*

Unnecessary pain is suffering that goes beyond the core emotional response. It is exaggerated, intensified, and prolonged suffering which generally is due to extremely self-critical thinking. In the wake of a seriously distressing personal event, many people launch into a ruthless attack on the self, either with actual statements spoken aloud to others, or with private inner thoughts and beliefs. Examples of this include, "I'm so stupid," "I'm so screwed up," "Nothing I do is right," "What the hell is wrong with me?!" "I'm being silly and childish to feel so upset about this," "I hate myself."

An almost-constant inner barrage of self-condemning thoughts represents one of the most common sources of human emotional suffering. While facing the truth of "necessary pain" is probably essential to successful emotional healing, unnecessary pain only intensifies and prolongs suffering.

One way to distinguish between necessary and unnecessary pain is to ask some basic questions: Even though this emotional pain hurts a lot, is it understandable? In some way does it make sense to me that I'm feeling this way, given the fact that I'm going through a very stressful time in my life? Does this pain lead me to take corrective action? Does expressing the pain result in any sense of relief/release? Does it bring me into closer contact with loved ones?

Of course, sometimes these are difficult questions to answer with certainty, since a good deal of necessary pain initially hurts so much that it's hard to imagine that it can serve any helpful purpose.

"For a long time after my divorce, I kept saying to myself, 'You've gotta get over this!' ... But eventually it dawned on me... how is a person supposed to feel after her husband leaves her?! Of course, this hurts like hell. It's normal to feel upset."

An important facet of most courses of brief therapy is to help you sort through inner feelings and thoughts... to confront, feel, acknowledge your legitimate necessary pain, while learning effective ways to stem the tide of inner self-criticism. (We'll talk a lot about strategies for reducing self-criticism in Chapter 13).

9: From Talk that Hurts to Talk that Heals

"How can talking help?"

Good question. You may be thinking, "I've already talked about this problem a lot... What good will it do to go in and talk to a shrink about it?" or "I've talked this to death... I don't see how just talking about it again would help."

Let's be clear, *some types of talking aren't helpful* and, in fact, some kinds of talking about emotionally difficult issues can increase your despair and just make matters worse! So to begin our understanding of how talk therapy works and how it can help, let's consider three types of talking: talk that hurts, talk that hides, and — in the next chapter — talk that heals.

Talk that Hurts

It's worth repeating: some kinds of talking about emotionally difficult issues can increase your despair and just make matters worse! Three very common kinds of talking that often occur during stressful times virtually guarantee you'll suffer even more. Talk like this (whether it's actually spoken aloud or just "self-talk" in your head) works like a pain amplifier, turning up the volume on the intensity of emotional pain.

The first hurtful style is *making extremely derogatory and critical comments about yourself.* We spoke about this in Chapter 8 as a source of unnecessary pain.

A second form of hurtful talk is *jumping to inaccurate or unrealistic conclusions.* Such conclusions may suggest extreme calamities ("I'm falling apart... I am *completely* out of control!"), or all-or-none statements ("Absolutely nothing I do is right!"). You may be making some poor decisions or mistakes, but you're certainly not 100% wrong about everything. This kind of talk just intensifies your idea that you are helpless and powerless — it's like throwing gasoline on your "distress fire."

The third common self-destructive talk is *making extremely negative predictions.* For example, concluding that the very worst possible outcome *absolutely will* happen.

When these types of talking dominate, then in a real sense, talking does not help (we will share with you ways to actively change these kinds of negative self-talk in Chapters 13 and 17).

Talk that Hides

Many kinds of talk also take people far away from their honest inner emotions. Language can help us avoid or distort the truth. Let's look at several examples.

Quick Closure

"Yes, I know it's bad, but I'll get over it... Did you see the
  NBA playoff game last night?"

Minimizing
  "Oh, it's not that bad."
  "Other people have gone through worse things. I shouldn't
    complain."
  "I feel sad, but I'm OK. I can handle it."
Injunctions
  "I need to be strong."
  "I shouldn't cry."
  "I can't get so emotional... I've got to get myself under
    control."
Outright Denial
  "I'm not upset. I'm... (sob)... OK."

In each of these cases, the words (or inner thoughts) direct your
focus away from inner emotions or the awareness of painful realities.
Sometimes this process is temporarily helpful, especially when
you're feeling very overwhelmed. These natural human maneuvers
are designed to protect us from too much pain. But this defensive
stance can backfire and result in excessive blocking of honest
emotions. Healing is stopped in its tracks.

So how can talking help you heal? We'll see in the next chapter.

10: From Confusion to Clarity

Sometimes it seems we talk ourselves into emotional difficulty.
Can we also talk ourselves out of it?

Only if we're really careful about *how* we talk...

Talk that Heals

Talking out loud about important thoughts, feelings and
experiences can be one of the most effective and rapid ways to "get
clear" about your emotions — unless of course it's the sort of talk

we discussed in the previous chapter. If the talking is done in a safe and supportive relationship with a therapist, the chances are excellent that it can lead to healing.

An emotional crisis can bring on lots of vague, ill-defined, disturbing emotions and sensations. It's easy to feel confused and unclear during these times. You may notice an intense uneasiness or tension in your body, a lump in your throat or tightness in your stomach. The confusing mix of emotions may only intensify anxiety, uncertainty and helplessness.

If you're able to talk with an understanding person about your thoughts, feelings and experiences, life often starts to make sense, bit-by-bit. You make connections between events and your feelings. It's as if you're shining a light into a dark cellar, gradually seeing more clearly what's inside.

We humans don't like feeling uncertain and confused. As we gain clarity and understanding, we feel a greater sense of mastery and control. Talking — describing your emotions — often makes vague feelings concrete, and can help you understand them better.

Shawna's situation offers an example. She feels distant and alone in her marriage, as Tim has become increasingly preoccupied with work. The intimacy in their relationship has evaporated, and she is more and more sad and lonely. Here's a sample dialog from one of her therapy sessions:

Shawna: *Today at work for no reason, I started crying. It was crazy. Nothing bad happened. What's wrong with me?*

Therapist: *Well, let's look at what was happening today. What went on in the office?*

Shawna: *Nothing really.*

Therapist: *Well, maybe it will help if we go over it together. Tell me about today.*

Shawna: *I was at work. My girlfriend, Diane, was talking about her love relationship and how it wasn't working out. She's talked about it before, but all of a sudden for no reason, I just started feeling terrible. I felt like I was going to cry... I'm not all that interested in her love life...*

Therapist: *You were starting to cry?*

Shawna: *Yeah.* (She looks sad.)

Therapist: *I wonder if there was something about your conversation with her that struck a chord within you... Tell me what comes to your mind.*

Shawna: *Well, I guess I thought, "Yeah, I know how you feel... Things never work out for me either. I'm married and I'm unhappy."* (She starts to cry.)

Therapist: *That hurts... Do your tears make sense?*

Shawna: *Yes.*

In a brief interchange about the events of the day, the meaning and source of Shawna's pain became clear to her. This is not a fancy psychotherapeutic technique nor is it magical. People help other people do this sort of thing all the time: one person listens and encourages another person to talk. Many therapists take this approach: "Let's see what's happened... I bet we can make sense of this." By *asking questions,* by *listening* and *encouraging talking* the therapist helps the client become aware of the personal meaning of events and emotions.

If the therapist had said, "I'm sure it was nothing," or "Well, you're over it now," or "It was probably just PMS," the process would have been quickly ended. Shawna would be just as much in the dark as before the session.

Shawna had initially tried to close the door by answering "Nothing really," to the therapist's inquiry, "Can you tell me what went on in the office?" The therapist nudged it open again, and she started to talk.

This is not just *talking* or "chit-chat." The goal is *understanding,* discovering true feelings, finding out what's really important. In this case, Shawna's sadness and confusion were replaced with greater understanding. As she became more aware of her own emotional turmoil, her feelings of sadness became an important issue for her to explore.

The talking helped Shawna open emotional doors, get in touch with her true feelings, understand herself better, view reality more clearly. Her choices and actions won't always turn out right, but they'll be more "in sync" with her genuine needs, beliefs and values. That gives her the best shot at emotional health.

More Ways Talk Can Help

In times of emotional distress, you may take things personally, quickly arrive at broad conclusions, and fail to notice important details. This process leads to lots of errors.

Let's listen to Oscar, a 21-year-old college student, in conversation with his therapist:

Oscar: *I was talking with my mother on the phone last night, trying to tell her about breaking up with Shelley. By the time I got off the phone, I felt terrible... I don't know, I just have a hard time getting along with my mom. Other people seem to have a good connection with their parents. What's wrong with me?*

Let's take a closer look for a moment. Oscar is upset, and the conversation with his mother left him feeling worse. Part of his upset is from the recent breakup of a romance, part of it is from his disappointment about the phone conversation, but most of it comes from his belief about himself ("What's wrong with *me?*").

In therapy, Oscar's therapist asked him to tell the story again, but to give more specifics. Oscar responded, *"There's not much more to say. I felt lousy after the call, and that's that.*

Oscar is doing what many of us do — he comes up with a fairly brief version of an event (a version that may neglect or ignore important elements). Let's see how the therapist helps Oscar to talk about this event in a different way.

Therapist: *It sounds as though you felt really disappointed after talking with your mom.*

Oscar: *Right.*

Therapist: *I'd like to ask you to tell me about it again, but this time, slow down... take your time. Share with me some more details. Ok?*

Oscar: *...uh, ok...*(long pause). *I said to her that Shelley had just told me she'd gone out with another guy... and it just tore me up to hear that.*

Therapist: *What did your mom say to you then?*

Oscar: (pauses) ...*She said "Well, son, these things happen. You'll get over it." And then she sorta changed the subject.*

Therapist: *Well, how was that for you to hear?*

Oscar: *I guess she's right...*

Therapist: *Well, maybe, but I want to ask you, at that moment when she said "these things happen" how did you feel?... What did you notice in that moment?*

Oscar: (pauses)... *I felt real let down, real sad.*

Therapist: *Why do you think?... What was it in her words that might have touched on a feeling with you?*

Oscar: *I was calling to get support... I wanted her to know how upset and sad I've been...*

Therapist: *You wanted her to be there for you.*

Oscar: *Yeah, ...and this has happened before with her. She just doesn't listen. Oh, she says she cares, but sometimes I wonder.*

Therapist: *You were reaching out to her and telling her about your feelings... and she didn't really hear you?*

Oscar: *Not at all... She was acting like it was no big deal... but it is a big deal! This is probably the worst time of my life and she doesn't get it!*

Therapist: *You said at the end of the phone call you thought, "What's wrong with me?" What are you thinking right now?*

Oscar: *I don't think there's anything actually wrong with me, I think I was mostly upset because she didn't seem to hear me... or to care.*

What's really going on here in this two-minute dialog? Initially, Oscar thought the problem was "him"; he had a negative view of himself: "Something's wrong with me." He's lost Shelley, he isn't communicating with his mother, and he's down on himself. The therapist's encouragement helped Oscar to slow down and talk about the events as they unfolded, and *to notice how he felt*. In Oscar's conversation with his therapist he was able to increase his *awareness* — to pay attention to, to notice, and to acknowledge his emotional reactions — and he explored the *personal meaning* of the event — what losing Shelley *meant* to him.

As Oscar became more clear about what actually happened during the conversation with his mother, and how he really felt, he changed his view of himself. This is a very important change. His self-perception shifted from "There must be something wrong with me," to "I was sad, I was reaching out. It's understandable for someone at a time like this to look for support. It's not so much that there is something wrong with me. It's that my mother was unable or unwilling to really hear my pain."

Oscar has a lot of sadness and grief. He doesn't need to increase his distress by making unrealistic negative assumptions about himself. Unlike talking with his mother, talking with his therapist helped turn around his attitude toward himself.

Talking like this — exploring events realistically, clarifying feelings, gaining understanding — is a powerful way to change your view of a situation and can significantly reduce unnecessary pain. This is talk that heals, and paves the way for positive attitudes and actions in your life.

11: From Illusion to Reality

Reality for each of us is influenced by what other people tell us: "Your father is a good man." "You know, your mother really does love you." "I really want to spend more time with you honey, but I have a lot of work to do." "I'm doing this for your own good." "Of course I love you. I don't have to *tell* you ... you should *know* it!"

Views of reality are also shaped by injunctions: "Don't rock the boat," "Don't be so sensitive," "I should like my job; it pays well," "I shouldn't complain; others have it a lot worse than I do."

Some mental health professionals believe that this kind of thinking occurs in the conscious and logical part of the mind. This "external" view of reality (beliefs told to you by others) tends to dominate conscious awareness and constitutes what we will call "Version

One" of reality. Sometimes Version One may be accurate; sometimes not.

On another level, we may perceive, think about and respond to the world in a very different way. This level is based much more on direct experiences, intuitions, sensations and feelings — a more immediate, gut-level response to what's happening in the moment. These perceptions and responses have little to do with what we have been told by others to think or believe. Rather they come naturally from within the self — a type of inner truth. We refer to this "internal" view as "Version Two."

Versions One and Two may differ. Years ago, during her first menstrual period, Beth complained to her mother of painful cramping. Her mother responded, "You're too young to have a period!" The young girl was now confronted with conflicting views of reality: Mom's view ("You are not having a period") and her own view ("I hurt"). A self-confident child might say, "Mom, you're wrong!" But many children will accept the mother's version of truth, and ignore the reality of their own experience.

> " 'Version One' of reality (beliefs told to you by others) tends to dominate conscious awareness... 'Version Two' is based on direct experiences, intuitions, feelings."

The internal reality of physical pain, emotions and needs can be ignored by thinking things like: "I'm making a big deal out of nothing," or "It's not that bad," or "Mom must know what's really happening." Or you can deny your feelings by blocking them from awareness — either partially or completely — leaving you out of touch with your inner reality.

Recall Shawna's story from the previous chapter. At first she didn't even notice her anger toward Tim. She just felt upset, afraid and tearful. For her, Version One meant, "Tim is a good man. He says he loves me. It could be worse." In therapy she began to listen more carefully to her inner experiences, and gradually became aware of her Version Two: "He's rarely at home. There is little intimacy. I feel empty, unhappy and angry. He says 'I love you,' but his behavior tells a different story."

Discovering the truth about her relationship with Tim brought Shawna closer to objective reality. Though she knew Version One was fashioned on empty promises, words, and her own strong hopes, she wanted desperately to believe it. But it wasn't true. As she talked and explored her feelings in therapy sessions, Version One faded and gave way to her real feelings. Tim may have had good intentions and sincerely believed that his words and promises of love were genuine. However, the "bottom-line" reality for Shawna was Version Two. She didn't like it, and it hurt, but it was real.

Check It Out!

Here are a couple of "reality checks" you can do to promote your own growth and emotional healing:

• *Question your own personal "Version Ones" regarding: important others* (parents, spouses, relatives, friends), *world views* ("The world is fair," "Bad things don't happen to good people,"), and *guidelines for living* ("Don't be emotional," "Don't be so sensitive," "Don't get angry").

- *Pay attention to your direct experience* — inner reactions, sensations, longings and emotions. Don't deny what you know is true.
  > *Facing the truth often means pain...*
  > *But doing so allows you to heal and grow!*

"The Truth Shall Make You Free"

The Biblical saying is proven every day by patients in therapy. Your truth cannot be defined or dictated from without, but must be discovered from within. Brief therapy can help.

When you make time to really talk about your thoughts, feelings and other inner experiences, one outcome is often an increased awareness of inner truths. "My childhood was not happy." "My father didn't truly show me love." "My job isn't gratifying." "My mother hurt me." "I feel a lack of closeness in my marriage." Such discoveries both hurt and help. You then must face and grieve the loss of illusions (e.g., the illusion of a happy childhood or a meaningful marriage).

Ultimately, Version Two may be okay. You may start to see your partner for who s/he really is. Maybe that's alright; maybe not. Accurate awareness may ignite open conflict or productive problem-solving in a relationship; it can lead to marital counseling or even to divorce. But increased awareness of inner truth may result in less confusion and a stronger sense of self.

Within each person there are many "truths," so the search is not aimed at finding "one truth," but at the discovery of all your beliefs, needs and emotions. It's a lifelong process, of course, but when you can begin to clarify these aspects of yourself, you can sort out who you are, figure out what problems you want to tackle and feel more solid about the actions you choose to take.

Brief therapy may be your most valuable resource as you find your way.

12: From Isolation to Contact

"**S**hared pain is easier to bear."

Well now, that depends on how your sharing is received by others. Sometimes opening up to another person can make matters worse, as is the case when the other person responds to the expression of emotion by *judging*. In contrast, sharing which is received with *acceptance and support* can contribute much to the healing process. In this chapter, we'll take a look at some helpful and some not-so-helpful conditions for sharing your pain.

Good Therapists Don't Judge

They do however, offer honest feedback... and a trained therapist knows the difference.

Friends sometimes will judge your feelings or actions in the name of "honest feedback" also. Their intentions may be constructive, but the result can be very destructive. Sometimes such judging is blatant; sometimes it is subtle, but it's almost never helpful.

Let's look at some examples:

Obvious Judgement

"You should be ashamed of yourself."

"You're being too emotional, too sensitive."

Disguised Judgement

"Now, now, don't cry."

"Look on the bright side."

"You need to put it behind you and get on with your life."

The obvious or underlying message implied is judgement: "It's wrong to feel that way," or "There is something wrong with you." In response, the person in pain may begin to feel ashamed or inadequate, and shut down emotionally. She is likely to become increasingly inhibited about sharing inner feelings, further cutting her off from connections with others. In such cases, sharing is hurtful rather than healing.

Other Types of Non-Helpful Sharing

Some listeners can't wait to jump in and offer brilliant insights or good advice. Sometimes this response is helpful, but often it is not. In fact, it generally closes the door on deeper emotional sharing.

Other listeners will attempt to convince you — and themselves — that they "understand." True understanding is hard to achieve. When the listener rather quickly or in a phony, shallow way says, "I understand," that's usually a type of non-helpful sharing. People are just so unique and so complex in their make-up that to come even close to a state of true understanding requires a *lot* of listening and a good deal of time spent coming to know the other person. The friend who says, "I understand," is probably trying to be helpful and trying to express care and concern. However, the person sharing her pain often thinks, "How can she really understand?" The result again is a closing down of emotion and a reluctance to share.

> *"It takes two to speak the truth — one to speak and another to hear."*
> — Henry David Thoreau

Brief therapy offers a safe place to share emotional experiences and feelings with another person in a non-judgmental and supportive atmosphere.

Benefits of Positive Sharing

When sharing pain with another person, you may *experience strong emotions* that otherwise would seem completely overwhelming. The other person can be like an anchor, providing some degree of stability and strength, thus lessening the intensity of your emotions.

A crisis may call up a host of emotions, some too intense, some too shameful to handle alone. An extremely valuable consequence of having the opportunity to discuss your feelings with a therapist is *feeling more "OK" about having human emotions.* As an understanding person listens to and accepts you, you may begin to feel less guilt, less shame and disturbing emotions begin to seem more normal and understandable. Many people are afraid that others will be disgusted, or shocked, or critical when they reveal deep inner feelings, but a tremendous sense of relief can result when you see that another person hears you and does not condemn you.

Sharing pain with another also gives you *a chance to talk out loud about your feelings.* We discussed the value of talking in Chapters 9 and 10. People can, and do, talk to themselves, of course, but talking is more effective when another person listens. It's an easier way to notice more clearly just what you're thinking, and how you're feeling.

Finally, and very importantly, sharing allows you simply to *be with another human being during a time of distress.* Most people feel any life crisis more acutely in isolation and aloneness. Being in contact with a therapist, a close friend, a loved one — even a stranger who is a good listener — can be soothing and healing.

Sharing pain connects us to one another. Compassion and love play an important role in the healing process.

Finally...

Brief psychotherapy isn't "just talk," or chit-chat. It's not hand-holding or an emotional crutch. Rather, it is important, emotionally difficult work, and serious endeavor. Psychotherapy, when the "chemistry" is right between client and therapist, helps people help themselves during hard times. Therapy is no longer seen so much as a "cure" for emotional illnesses as it is an effective way to facilitate growth, encourage effective coping and provide support when life is hard. Ultimately, psychotherapy works only when it helps people find their own strength.

The following chapters — "Part III: A Coping Skills Manual" — are designed to help you find your own strength. These ideas can be valuable both as aids to your brief therapy and as powerful self-help tools.

PART III
A Coping Skills Manual

"O.K. So I'm not crazy, it just feels that way. What do I do now? All these self-help books are the same; they say I've already learned everything, I just have to use what I know. Well, I'm too tired to care. Tell me something that I can do. I just don't think I can cope with all this."

Coping skills are not mysterious. Except for a few basic survival skills, you're not born with them — they're learned behaviors. Some people develop good coping and problem solving skills early in life, but some of us weren't that lucky. Life is unpredictable, and while sometimes the path is smooth and silky, most of us find a few rocks in the path from time to time (and occasionally an avalanche or two).

In this section of the book we will be sharing with you some very specific guidelines for effective coping. These strategies have been developed and refined by mental health professionals over the past two decades. Your therapist will probably introduce one or more of them as a part of your treatment. If not, we think you'll find them valuable self-help resources to complement and support your brief therapy.

Nothing fancy here; just solid action plans that can make a difference for people who are under stress. We'll focus on five areas: *cognitive coping skills* ("cognitive" refers to perceiving and thinking, thus this part will deal with ways to increase your ability to think clearly, problem solve and maintain a realistic perspective), *interpersonal problem solving and conflict resolution skills* (for effectively resolving difficulties with others), *staying healthy/ reducing stress* (keeping physically healthy can make a difference, especially during times of significant distress), self-monitoring *homework* (active ways to monitor your progress), and *strengthening your sense of self* (ways to feel more "solid" and self-confident).

These are skills almost anyone can develop, and they will help to lessen your emotional pain and give you back some sense of control over your feelings. They can increase the likelihood of success in brief therapy — and in your life beyond therapy.

13: "I think I can...I think I can..."

---- The Little Engine that Could

"*I want to go back to school so I can get a better paying job. But my youngest is having problems; his grades are dropping and his attitude is getting worse and worse. His father is no help at all!*"

Stephanie is a single mom with two teen-age boys, working at a dead-end job that barely lets her pay the bills.

"*I don't have medical coverage and can't afford a therapist for us. What am I supposed to do?! I could quit my job and get on welfare, then at least I'd have some medical care. But I don't want to do that. I want to go to school, but then I'd have even less time with the boys and they really need me now.*"

We're going to let you choose Stephanie's next line. Does she say,

"*I can't cope. I feel helpless... stuck. I can't deal with all this!*"
Or,

*"Things are really tough right now, but I've been through worse;
This is going to be hard, but I can handle it."*

Stephanie is, as the saying goes, "between a rock and a hard place." She knows she is facing a difficult time. However, if she *believes* she can cope, she may be distressed, but not overwhelmed — she'll feel more-or-less confident that she can manage.

On the other hand, if Stephanie begins to *think and believe*, "I can't cope," she'll feel more and more stress. Have her coping skills actually diminished? No. But her *self-confidence* is lessened if she doesn't *believe* she's able to handle the situation. Feelings of helplessness always increase distress.

How You Think Makes a Difference

We humans interpret our world through our *thoughts*, our *beliefs*, our *perceptions*, and our *attitudes*. By becoming aware of how your thoughts and attitudes influence your feelings, you can gain more control over your feelings — and your life.

Thoughts and attitudes are not mystical experiences. They naturally occur in our heads all the time — we're constantly "talking to ourselves," sometimes out loud, but more often silently. Your "self-talk" includes your observations of the world, conclusions, predictions and problem-solving. It happens very *automatically.* And that self-talk — your *thoughts* (ideas, beliefs, attitudes, opinions about yourself, others, the world) — can actually create positive or negative *feelings* (sadness, self-doubt, depression, anxiety, fear, anger, pain, discomfort, uncertainty...).

When you're faced with serious stressors or traumatic events, your self-talk is likely to become more negative ("I can't cope..." "Everything I do is wrong."), leading to low self-esteem and lack of confidence.

Your life — and the progress of your brief therapy — will improve if you can begin to turn your self-talk around. You can do that by paying attention to it, then taking action steps to change it.

Listen to Yourself

In order to get a handle on this thinking-feeling-action process, you'll need to start *paying attention* to what you are feeling and thinking. For example, you'll notice changes in your moods and feelings during therapy sessions. Your therapist will help by asking questions about how you're feeling, and what you think or believe about an event or person or life circumstance. The goal will be to spot unrealistic, negative or pessimistic thinking when it occurs.

As you begin to notice and recognize your thoughts and feelings you may actually find your feelings getting stronger. That's because for the first time in a long time you may actually be allowing yourself to feel them. Don't panic, it's normal!

How to Turn Your Negative Thinking Around

Please keep in mind that you don't have to change your whole personality to have an impact on negative thinking. All you have to do is a simple three-step process. It takes just a minute. *Step One:* Notice negative, automatic thoughts the moment they occur. Ask yourself, "I'm feeling upset right now... What's going through my mind? What am I thinking?" *Step Two:* Ask yourself — "Are my thoughts right now 100% accurate and realistic?" *Step Three:* Replace negative and/or unrealistic thoughts with thoughts that are more accurate. In the next few pages we'll

> *"Your life — and the progress of your brief therapy — will improve if you can begin to turn your self-talk around."*

elaborate on this simple process. Let's start by looking at an example.

Imagine you are asked to give a 20-minute presentation at work before a group of 50 people. You seriously dislike speaking in public; in fact, it terrifies you. You may begin thinking, moments before your talk, "Oh my God, look at all those people. I'm going to blow it! I'm going to start to shake, my voice is going to crack, and I'll forget my speech. I'll humiliate myself and they're going to think I'm stupid!" These all-too-common thoughts are good examples of the sort of self-talk that focuses largely on negative outcomes. Such pessimism can scare you and increase your experience of disaster, anxiety, and self-doubt.

If you were to think instead, "Oh my God, look at all those people. Now settle down. Sure I'm feeling anxious. Lots of people don't like public speaking and it's normal to be a little on edge about this, but I need to encourage and support myself. I'm going to give it my best. I may not win an Academy Award, but I'll get through this. I don't like this kind of stuff, but I'll survive. It may not be pleasant, but it won't kill me."

By replacing the negative thoughts with more realistic, appropriate, and supportive beliefs, you admit to your unpleasant feelings while giving yourself support. In doing so, you are also stemming the tide of negative thoughts. The last thing that you need to do prior to getting up to give a talk is to scare yourself! The stress will not be completely avoided, but the outcome will be quite different. Your silent but potent inner voice can have a tremendous effect on the amount of stress you experience and your feelings of self-confidence.

Challenge Your Thinking

You're saying, "OK. I can do that, but be more specific." Fair enough.

In this section, we've identified several common obstacles to healthy thinking, and some specific ways to challenge them. You can interrupt negative thinking if you'll stop and ask yourself a question that examines your thoughts. Look inside yourself and bring your thoughts into conscious awareness. Use your realistic thinking to make more positive thoughts and changes. The idea is to *identify* how your thoughts are upsetting you, then to *challenge* any faulty thinking and replace it with a healthier outlook. How many of these are part of your style?

- *Jumping to conclusions* ("I just know she thinks I'm a jerk," "I know I'm blowing this job interview... the interviewer looks bored to tears.") How can you know what others are thinking or feeling? No one can read another person's mind. Jumping to negative conclusions *always* increases distress. In such situations, it's helpful to ask yourself, "What do I *really* know about this situation?"

• *Predicting the worst possible outcome* ("This is going to be *horrible!*" "I'll *never* get over it.") Remind yourself that you can't tell the future. Then, ask yourself, "Where is the evidence that this terrible catastrophe is about to happen? What makes me think that this absolutely *will* happen?"

• *All-or-nothing thinking* (i.e., you make a mistake and then conclude, "I can't do *anything* right!"). Challenge directly with "Is that absolutely true? I can't do *anything* right?" List a few things you've done correctly. Then focus on the specific problem or mistake and acknowledge it.

• *Seeing the worst* (and ignoring the positive things). Remind yourself, "I need to look at the whole picture, including the good things, not just the things that go wrong."

• *Labeling* ("I'm an idiot.") You're not, or you wouldn't have come this far on your own. Like everybody else, you've done some dumb things in your life, and you will again. But "idiot" is a term with precise meaning (look it up). If you really were one, you wouldn't be reading this book — or any other. Other labels are similarly false. Keep in mind that you're a person who makes human mistakes — and is capable of human successes as well.

• *Unrealistic Self-Blame* ("It's all my fault.") Under stress it's common to get into excessive self-blame. But assuming 100% of the fault is probably not realistic and serves mainly to increase feelings of self-hatred and low self-esteem.

• *The "Shoulds"* (believing firmly that you or others *must* act only a certain way). Tell yourself that many things happen that are not pleasant, but this doesn't mean that they "should" or "shouldn't" be. It may be more helpful and less painful to rephrase your thought in terms of what you want, (e.g., "She should know how I feel." Instead, say to yourself, "I want her to understand, but she can't read my mind." or "This shouldn't be happening." Rephrase: "It is happening and I don't like it!")

The "shoulds" are an especially powerful negative thought pattern. When you think with "shoulds" you become a victim. Feelings of powerlessness and helplessness increase. Thinking with the "shoulds" is a way of strongly insisting that things must be a certain way. Thinking these thoughts never changes the reality — it only makes you feel worse.

An effective assault on the shoulds is to say to yourself, "Now wait a minute. It's not a matter of shoulds or shouldn'ts. My wife just left me and it really hurts. I don't like it one little bit!" By doing so, you are honestly stating how you feel and have become more accepting of yourself as being understandably in pain. (Ideas in this section draw on the work of Dr. David Burns, 1980.)

Tools to Build Coping Skills and Self-Confidence

Self-confidence is basically the ability to trust in your coping resources. Remember, that when self-confidence begins to sink, you may forget that you functioned successfully in the past. You may tend to focus on your failures. Instead, you might think, "I need to remember that I'm strong and have handled problems in the past. I need to believe in myself. It'll be hard at first, but I can do it."

The trick is not to try to fool yourself into believing that there are no risks or pain, or that you are completely without fault. Your goal is to acknowledge, accept, and gain perspective. Be positive, not self-critical. Recognize that your *thoughts* are making you feel more anxious or depressed. You're hurting yourself and you need to stop the negative thoughts. Actively replace your thoughts with positive coping statements (see list on page 54 for some samples which may fit you). Your self-confidence will begin to return.

Begin to challenge your thinking frequently. As soon as you notice an unpleasant feeling, reel it in, take a moment, write down the automatic thought along with a more realistic response. (Jotting these thoughts down on paper is an especially effective way to become clear about how you are thinking, and to then gain a more realistic perspective.) If you cannot do it on the spot, do it later in the day, taking a few minutes to go back over the events of the day and your thoughts. It takes a bit of time and effort to write things down, but the effects will be better if you bring your thoughts to awareness.

The strategies we've mentioned in this chapter actively interfere with negative thinking, and can be helpful in restoring your self-confidence to deal with the demands of life. These techniques are not magical solutions, they are straightforward actions you can take *now* and can practice between sessions of brief therapy. These cognitive coping skills have been shown to be some of the most rapid approaches to helping people regain control over unpleasant feelings. As you begin to feel better, you can develop more decision-making and problem-solving skills that will help you gain an even greater sense of self-mastery.

In the next chapter we'll focus on taking direct action to change stressful events that arise in important interpersonal relationships.

Positive Self-Statements to Help You Cope

1. This feeling isn't comfortable or pleasant, but I can accept it.
2. I can be in pain, sad, anxious, or... and still deal with this situation.
3. I can handle it.
4. This is not an emergency. It's OK to think slowly about what's happening and how I feel.
5. This is not the worst thing that could happen.
6. This will pass.
7. I don't have to let this get to me; I'll ride through it.
8. I deserve to feel okay.
9. I don't have to do it right the first time; I'm not perfect but neither is anybody else.
10. I'm having a feeling that I don't like, it won't hurt me, it just doesn't feel good.
11. These are just thoughts; I can change them.
12. I don't have to have all the answers, nobody else does either, though some folks think they do.
13. I have the right to change my mind about what I think about any given situation.
14. I have the right to make mistakes.
15. I have the right to feel anger.
16. I have the right to say "I don't know."
17. "I think I can, I think I can..."

14: Getting Along With Others

Broken promises, unfair treatment, obliviousness, insensitivity, attempts to control, manipulate or dominate, unwillingness or inability to compromise, emotional, physical or sexual abuse, harassment, dishonesty, guilt trips....

Relationships! Can't live with 'em, can't live without 'em. Whether it's relatives, friends, lovers or colleagues, the one thing you can count on is that relationships are not only a vital part of your existence, but one of life's biggest challenges.

And the differences! Values, style, needs, opinions, history, life circumstances, disposition, temperament... people are definitely not all the same! Under the best of circumstances our differences add excitement and stimulation, but they inevitably also contribute to frustration and upset. Problems seem an inevitable part of living.

Bells, Whistles, and Other Alarms

If you have experienced conflicts with others, you may recall some of your own feelings about this experience. Those feelings and your reactions to them have become a part of your own unique "early warning system" or alarm, alerting you of possible danger: "Something is wrong here."

One thing that's true about alarm systems is that they are most useful when you learn to work with them. You don't want to suffer too many false alarms, but when the alarm does go off, it's time to take action to prevent a difficult situation from becoming worse. The greater your understanding and practice with the alarm the more helpful it can potentially be.

Psychologists have come to understand a number of fairly common alarms — reactions that are important cues for us to pay attention to so we know it's time to work at resolving conflict in our relationships. Here are a few examples:

- *Pent-up Feelings.* Have a hard time being as direct and forthright as you would like? For a variety of reasons you may grit your teeth and keep your feelings to yourself. This "emotional constipation" can become quite limiting and uncomfortable, not only for you, but for others in your life.

- *Avoiding.* "If I don't confront it, if I put it off, maybe it will go away." Kind of like the ostrich who buries its head in the sand to avoid the stampede. Pretending "it's not there" may offer psychological respite in the moment — like the ostrich, you might luck out and not get run over — but in the middle of a stampede the odds aren't good. While fantasy and magical thinking can be fun and may provide the opportunity to practice in your mind's eye, they are rarely helpful in the long run.

- *Excuses, Apologies or Justification.* There may be a time to provide a short, simple, direct explanation of why you decided to do or not do something. However, if this occurs more than rarely, or if you often feel guilty and overly apologetic, it's time for a change.

- *Putting Yourself Last.* Unless you're in the league of Buddha, Gandhi or Jesus, putting yourself last works only occasionally. Every healthy relationship you find yourself in requires some degree of mutual give and take. It's not healthy to always put your own needs last or constantly give in to others at your own expense. We're not suggesting that you adopt the opposite extreme — always putting yourself first — but we want you to recognize that the "middle ground," involving mutual support and acceptance, will generally result in stronger, more vital relationships.

- *Putting Yourself Down.* Do you ever hear yourself or someone you know say something like, "This may sound stupid, but...," or "I'm sorry to disagree, but..."? When you think, feel or express negative beliefs about yourself, you not only put yourself down, you increase the likelihood of staying stuck, and minimize your options and possibilities for change. If you believe only the worst about yourself, it's time to develop a more reasonable, balanced perspective.

• *Aggressive or Hostile Behavior.* Do you find yourself exploding inside or toward others? Would people describe you as hostile and aggressive? It's normal and natural to feel angry and upset at various points in life, but to take it out on yourself or others can be destructive.

Aggression is a style of expressing feelings that rarely takes others' feelings into consideration. Some folks learned this style while growing up, and may believe it is the only way they can feel powerful or in control of a situation or relationship. While there are many circumstances that need to be dealt with directly — including expressing such negative feelings as anger or upset — it is rarely, if ever, more effective to express feelings aggressively rather than assertively.

If you tend to be aggressive, your intimate relationships — if you're lucky enough to still have any — suffer. While you may attempt to deny it, this can result in a vicious circle of isolation and upset in which your aggressive feelings drive others away, resulting in you feeling even more angry and potentially aggressive.

• *Passive Self-Denial.* This style of dealing with others is also described as "timid" or "passive." While it is normal not to have strong feelings about *everything* in your life, it is not normal to pretend you don't have strong feelings about *anything.* This "whatever...," shrug-the-shoulders style is typical of those who are afraid to be honest with themselves or others about how they feel. If this is true of you, it may be your secret hope that if you avoid being assertive you can minimize the discomfort you associate with conflict. You may have learned to live with more unhappiness in your life than necessary. The long-term cost of self-denial is enormously high, including increased vulnerability to possible aggressive and abusive relationships.

Now that we've examined some unhealthy ways to deal with others, let's move on to a more reasonable, adaptive way of getting along, by expressing your feelings in a direct, appropriately *assertive* way.

Healthy Assertive Coping

If you find your relationships less than satisfying or even downright disappointing or painful, it may be that you've been following one or more of the unhealthy paths we've just discussed. If you want to be happier and feel more in control of your life, most therapists will recommend that you learn to become more assertive. That may sound a little scary at first, but please read on. We think you'll want to try it.

> *Being assertive means being able to choose how you will act in any given relationship situation.*

Assertiveness is a word most of us have heard but may not really understand. Common usage often gives the mistaken idea that being assertive is the same as being aggressive. Both styles do involve expressing important feelings without holding back, but assertiveness tempers honesty with genuine concern, sensitivity, and respect for the other person's feelings. Assertiveness is a style of expression that is equally comfortable with both negative and positive feelings.

You've seen people who appear totally comfortable in social situations, but the fact is that nobody's *born* assertive. Assertion is a learned style that involves developing healthy attitudes, overcoming some obstacles (such as anxiety), and learning a few effective behavioral skills. Being assertive means being able to *choose* how you will act in any given relationship situation.

It takes lots of practice to feel comfortable and natural when being assertive. Even if you're shy, even if you're not as confident as you would like, it's possible to learn to be assertive. Those who have developed the skill report more satisfying relationships and increased self-confidence.

Getting Started

The most important thing to remember about assertiveness is that it's a matter of *choice*. You needn't try to be assertive all the time. The first step is to look at a particular problem situation and very honestly ask yourself, "Is this important enough to justify action?" There are lots of times when it's honestly no big deal — a passive stance may be fine. However, we want to caution you about something: everyone encounters situations that in fact *are* very important, but some folks tell themselves, "It's no big deal," even when it really matters. So it's essential that you look at situations very honestly and realistically, and prepare yourself to take assertive action when it counts.

Goals of Assertive Conflict Resolution

One goal of acting assertively, of course, is to bring about a *change in a situation or in another person's behavior.* For example, if somebody is taking advantage of you, your goal might be, "I want him to stop doing this."

A second very important goal is to *increase your own self-respect.* We want to strongly emphasize that the second goal — increasing your own self-respect — really is the major goal in being assertive. Before you go to talk with somebody about an important issue, it's very helpful to remind yourself of these two goals and to tell yourself, "Obviously I want to make a change in the situation — I'm going in there to request a change. But regardless of what happens, I'm going to take this opportunity to express how *I* feel and what *my* opinions are. Even if_____doesn't give me what I want, I'm going to state my feelings and opinions firmly, and then I'm going to be able to walk out of there with my head held high."

Consider the Risks

"What are the realistic risks of being assertive?" Consider that question very consciously. You may imagine all sorts of very dangerous or upsetting consequences of acting assertively. These assumptions about "what's going to happen" actually may govern whether or not you act assertively. Sometimes unpleasant things do happen, of course, and we need to examine closely, honestly, and realistically what these risks may be.

Let's take a look at a few:

• *"The other person might become upset or angry or hurt or rejected."* Many people put off dealing with and confronting problem situations in relationships because they are afraid the other person is going to become extremely upset. The reality is that by avoiding the situation, you may perpetuate serious interpersonal problems for months or even for years— which could take a tremendous emotional toll on both of you. People tend to greatly overestimate the amount of emotional upset that actually may result when they confront another person. By-and-large, if you approach the other person honestly as an adult, treating her with respect, showing some sensitivity to her feelings, and just being honest with her — without belittling her or putting her down — any upset that does occur will be very short term. Deciding to confront the issue and deal with a temporary upset may be the first step toward permanent resolution.

• *"The other person may find a way to get back at me or to get even."* We want to caution you that being assertive is no guarantee that the other person is going to respond in a positive way. It would be great if every time you were assertive, the other person said, "Oh, that's fine. I understand." Sometimes that happens. Sometimes people are somewhat irritated or upset, but these feelings pass — they're temporary. And in some situations being assertive with certain kinds of people can lead to some very serious problems. This is often the case if you are dealing with an emotionally unstable or immature person. A very good example of this might be confronting a supervisor or boss who tends to be quite emotionally immature and who may, in fact, not like having an employee who is simply honest, direct and adult. Some insecure people in these kinds of positions enjoy and gain satisfaction from dominating and controlling other people; their focus is making sure that people under them are submissive and not assertive. With a person like this, you potentially risk getting seriously hurt, sometimes physically, and many times in non-physical ways that can be very damaging. (Losing your job comes to mind.) You have to use your head about this possibility by asking yourself, "What do I know about this person? Based on my experience, do I feel that this person is mature enough to endure and to handle an honest confrontation?" Sometimes the answer is "No, he's not." In that case, it may pay to *choose* to be non-assertive.

• *"The assertion may fail."* You may stick your neck out, you may ask for something, you may confront someone, and she may say, "Forget it! No way!" Many people are very afraid to look foolish or to feel helpless or not to know what to do should the assertion fail. One response you may wish to consider in such a situation is to respond quickly, "I'm sorry you feel that way. This issue is very important to me, and I hope you'll give some thought to what I've said."

(Shortly, we will be giving you some additional helpful "backup plans" for these situations. When you have decided to approach a problem situation in which there's even a slight chance that the assertion might fail, having some pre-arranged back-up plans is important: "What am I going to do if the assertion doesn't work?")

Risk vs. Reward: Short Run and Long Run

It's natural for people to tend to focus on the immediate emotional issues that might come up when they confront others and talk to them assertively. We think it's important for you to ask yourself, "Okay, I need to consider that, in fact, this other person might feel sad or might feel irritated or might get angry with me at the moment. But let me think about the long-term consequences of these responses. What do I think really will happen in the long run? Is she going to continue to be *very* sad or *very* upset for a prolonged time if I confront her?" Consciously appreciating this view, that negative responses may be short-term, can make the decision to be assertive easier.

Considering the longer-term positive consequences is also helpful. What may be going on inside your head when you think about being assertive are the short-term negative consequences. But we think it's very important as you're preparing to assert yourself to ask yourself, "Once I get through with this, even though there may be some upset, I wonder what the *positive results* could be?" These positive outcomes might be seen in terms of both the situation and yourself. You might ask yourself, "I wonder if maybe in the long run this decision to be assertive will solve the problem? Maybe this problem is something we won't have to deal with over and over and over again. Maybe I'm not going to be walking around with this pent-up anger and resentment all the time. It might make it easier for me to really get in and work on our relationship, to truly feel better about things." Another positive consequence would be that, "These people are going to know where I stand. Maybe they'll think twice before they try to take advantage of me again. I'm not a person who is willing to be pushed around; I'm going to stand up for myself."

Here's another positive result: "Even though this might be tough in some ways, just maybe after I've been assertive, I can walk out of there and tell myself, 'By gosh, you know what? I did that! I'm proud of myself!'"

Planning for Action

Systematically going over each of the steps mentioned above, in your own mind, can be very helpful. It is a way to prepare yourself emotionally and to get to a place of feeling okay about your decision to speak out. In addition, especially if the situation is very important to you or very emotional, it also may be helpful to write out exactly what you're going to say to the person ahead of time, and then to practice out loud several times, until you are expressing your thoughts in a way that feels right. If you have a trustworthy, close friend, you may wish to practice with him or her; let your friend pretend to be the other person as you practice and practice again.

Practicing an assertive response even two or three times can make a big difference in feeling okay about how you're coming across. If no one is available to help you, practicing in front of a mirror can be helpful, too, because it gives you an opportunity to watch and hear yourself and then to make some improvements. Then, when you are actually getting ready for the meeting, you already know how you're going to come across. (If you have the luxury of a video camera, that's an even better tool to help you practice and improve.)

Key Ingredients of Assertive Behavior

When Shawna decided to tell Tim about how she felt, she made a point to have his full attention. She started by stating, "This is very important to me, and I'd like you to listen to what I have to say." She also consciously made herself look directly into his eyes and began to talk in a firm, but non-hostile voice. "I think I have said the same words to him a hundred times, but this time he heard me. It wasn't what I said as much as how I said it. He got the message that I meant business."

As we consider what being assertive "looks like," and what the different aspects of assertion actually are, it's helpful to break assertive behavior down into three component parts:

• *Verbal content.* This refers to the particular words that you choose to speak, what you decide to say. There are two guidelines that you can use to make sure your verbal content is assertive; one is K I S S which stands for "*K*eep *I*t *S*hort and *S*imple." Many times when people are trying to be assertive, they get sidetracked, get off onto some long explanations, excuses, justifications, apologies and so forth. Getting to the point as quickly as possible will really pay off.

The second point about content is something called "I Language." When you're expressing what you feel, it's an effective strategy to say, "This is how *I* feel." Lots of times people inadvertently will say, "*You make me* feel sad," "*You make me* feel unhappy," "*You make me* feel angry" and so forth. This approach can present some problems; when you say "*You make me* feel...," in a sense, you're casting yourself in the role of a helpless person. And this role can increase feelings of anxiety and insecurity. There's simply something about saying, "*I* feel sad," or "*I* feel angry" that helps the message come across as more powerful. What's more, you're maintaining more self-control. Saying, "Look, *I* feel this way," actually increases and enhances your self-esteem and self-respect. Also, if you say to another person, "You make me feel" a certain way, that tends to greatly increase defensiveness. If you want to talk with others and negotiate for change or confront them about their behavior, statements that increase defensiveness decrease the chances of success. People simply tend to be more responsive and open to hearing someone say, "*I* feel sad," "*I* feel angry," and so forth. Take responsibility for your own feelings by using I language.

• *Vocal tone.* An assertive vocal tone is firm and direct. You're not coming across in an overly loud voice, which might scare people or make them feel you're aggressive, or, by contrast, in a silent, meek, whiny kind of voice. A firm, solid, well-modulated tone of voice conveys "I mean what I'm saying."

• *Gestures, Body Language and Eye Contact.* Probably the most important non-verbal element of communication is eye contact. When people are afraid, anxious or non-assertive, it's tough to make eye contact. Just watch the next time someone's talking to you and feeling anxious. There's something powerful and convincing about looking someone right in the eye and saying, "Hey, this is how I feel; this is my opinion." It's a non-verbal message that lets people know, "I mean what I'm saying."

Back-up Plans

In the real world, there are times when your assertions don't work the way you hoped.

The other person may respond in ways designed to get you to back off. Let's say that you're confronting someone about a very emotionally charged situation in which a lot of your feelings are being revealed. Some people will respond by saying, "You're just too emotional about this!" or "It's just like a woman to be so emotional!" One way to respond to this is to say, "You know what? I *do* have strong feelings about this issue, and I am going to make my point again." Then jump right back in and re-assert yourself. Reasserting your point in spite of the other person's response is a very effective way of stopping the other person from using this type of manipulation. You have not agreed that you are *too* emotional. You have simply affirmed your strong feelings.

The other person may respond to your assertion with tears and a lot of guilt messages. One way to deal with this is to say, "I know this is hard to hear, I know this is causing you pain, but this issue is important, and I want to repeat myself because we're going to work together and resolve this." Again, what you've done is to stop the other's attempt to use guilt to get you to back off from your assertive response.

> *"I know this is hard to hear... but this issue is important ... we're going to work together and resolve this."*

Some people may quibble with you about the legitimacy of what you feel. You have the right to state feelings and opinions without justifying them. One way to react to this response is to say, "Regardless of the reasons, this is my opinion," or "Well, let's face it, we may not agree on this, but all the same, this is how *I* feel." Again, you're re-asserting yourself and not bowing to the demand for justifications.

When dealing with an extremely angry or aggressive person, it can be helpful to say, "I can see that you're very angry and upset, but it's important that we resolve this issue, and we are going to talk about this. If we can't talk about it now, that's okay. But I'm going to come back, and we're going to talk about it later."

Is It Time for Action in Your Real World?

We hope you'll find this discussion about assertion helpful. Deciding to confront truly difficult interpersonal problems and act in an assertive way is often hard to do and may be accompanied by a good deal of uneasiness, and sometimes actual risks. Many people have found it helpful to seek out an assertiveness training group — a type of group therapy that helps people learn how to act in an assertive way, provides opportunities for practice and role playing, and offers support. Many have benefited by reading the excellent self-help books on assertion which we have listed in the References section of this book. And working directly with your therapist can be valuable — particularly if you are preparing to resolve significant problems in important relationships. The therapist can provide guidance and support.

As you might guess, becoming assertive takes hard work and lots of practice. Many of us have to unlearn behavior we have practiced for years and learn new healthier behavior and attitudes in its place, then practice, practice, practice. Fortunately, assertiveness training has flourished and it's likely that you'll find workshops covered by your insurance benefit or sponsored by a number of organizations in your community.

Dealing with really significant conflicts with others can be incredibly difficult. That's a reality which has to be acknowledged. At the same time, the approaches advocated in this chapter have been in wide use during the past twenty years and have a solid track record. Being assertive is no panacea for resolving the emotionally-charged conflicts in your life, but it certainly is an approach that has a good chance of success.

You have a right to say *no* to emotional abuse, to express your own feelings, and to ask for changes in another's behavior. We encourage you to learn to be assertive.

15: Staying Healthy/Reducing Stress

As you think about how brief therapy may help you deal with emotional distress, consider this: *Physical problems often cause emotional distress, and emotional upsets may produce physical symptoms.* In this chapter, we'll take a close look at how you can reduce emotional stress by keeping yourself physically well and learning to relax.

Stressful life events often bring on very unpleasant and sometimes painful or dangerous physical symptoms including tension headaches, insomnia, fatigue, restlessness, loss of sex drive, ulcers, high blood pressure and decreased energy. Recent evidence suggests that prolonged, significant emotional distress can also impair the functioning of the immune system, increasing your risk of certain infectious diseases, retarding recovery from physical illnesses and, in extreme cases, opening the door for the development of cancer.

Three primary approaches have been shown to be quite effective in reducing some of the physical symptoms associated with life stress: *changing unhealthy habits, relaxation,* and *appropriate use of medications.*

Change Unhealthy Habits

Research has shown over and over again that under the impact of emotional distress, people develop bad habits, including excessive use of alcohol, tobacco, caffeine and junk foods. These poor nutritional and health habits can, in the long run, result in serious physical illnesses, such as cardiac disease and cancer. There are a host of short-term risks as well.

Alcohol: Arguably the most used — and abused — drug in the United States, alcohol can provide a very potent and quick sense of release from physical tension and can promote a temporary feeling of euphoria or relaxation. Many people who are experiencing emotional pain seek the quick relief alcohol provides. While we don't intend to be moralistic about the issues of alcohol use, the evidence clearly shows that the use of alcohol can backfire, especially over a prolonged period of time on a regular basis and in high amounts.

Alcohol, in and of itself, is responsible for tremendous aggravation of the symptoms of depression and anxiety. However, alcohol is a seductive substance; because the immediate result of drinking is relief, the person perceives that the alcohol is helpful. But prolonged use actually results in a change in the neurochemistry of the brain, *increasing* — not relieving — anxiety and depression. Avoiding, reducing or eliminating alcohol intake during stressful times is one key self-care action that you can take. (*Note: If you have been drinking heavily, it is important to know that abrupt discontinuation of alcohol can result in very unpleasant and sometimes dangerous withdrawal symptoms. Such discontinuation should only be done under medical supervision.*)

Caffeine: This widely-used drug is found in some unexpected places: in coffee, of course, and in a host of other substances that people consume, including tea, certain drinks (especially colas), and — horrors! — *chocolate;* in a number of pain medications (e.g., Excedrin); in a number of diet pills. Like alcohol, caffeine is a seductive drug. One common physical effect of stress is a sense of fatigue and decreased energy. Caffeine is a potent stimulant and can provide, rather quickly, a sense of improved alertness and energy. Some researchers believe that caffeine has mild anti-depressant effects and thus may be used by some chronically depressed people to elevate their moods.

Caffeine also can backfire. Studies of caffeine use and abuse indicate that when people ingest more than 250 mg. per day of caffeine, there is a significant likelihood of developing such stress-related symptoms as jitteriness, tension, anxiety and insomnia. The risks of symptoms increase dramatically when the amount of caffeine surpasses 500 mg. per day. (The average cup of coffee contains approximately 150 mg. of caffeine, and the typical cola drink or tea contains around 50 mg. of caffeine.)

Another often unrecognized but important symptom of caffeine use is disruption of the quality of sleep. Even if you're able to go to sleep, large amounts of caffeine may produce significantly more restless sleep. As a result, you'll fail to get adequate rest during the night, which leads to excessive day-time fatigue. To combat this fatigue, the typical coffee/cola drinker chooses — you guessed it — to drink more caffeine.

In difficult times, it may seem silly to worry about the amount of coffee you're drinking. Many people "pooh-pooh" the notion that caffeine contributes to emotional problems, but clinical research shows that caffeine can cause or exacerbate stress-related symptoms.

The bottom line here: *One decisive action you can take during times of stress is to reduce or eliminate caffeine.* Note that if you are accustomed to drinking large amounts of caffeine, and you quit "cold turkey," you will likely experience significant caffeine withdrawal symptoms: anxiety, restlessness, tension and headaches. Thus, if you have become accustomed to ingesting large amounts of caffeine, you'll want to *gradually* decrease your intake of caffeine over the period to two to three weeks, progressively replacing caffeinated beverages with decaffeinated beverages.

Exercise: At times of great emotional distress, you may experience a tremendous sense of decreased energy and fatigue. And during such times, motivating yourself to engage in normal physical exercise becomes even more difficult. You'll probably feel like stopping your normal exercise program, perhaps reducing your normal daily activity level as well. Don't do it. Fatigue feeds on itself. The more tired you feel, the more you're inclined to sit on the couch or lie in bed. However, reduced activity almost always leads to a progressive cycle of increasing fatigue.

Another common outcome of emotional distress is significant weight gain because of decreased activity and an increased appetite for inappropriate foods. Weight gain can have negative consequences for both physical functioning and emotional well-being. Significant weight gain may lead to feelings of inadequacy, low self-esteem, obesity, hypertension and diabetes.

An important decision you can make during difficult times of emotional distress is to take care of yourself as best you can, focusing on proper nutrition, exercise and a reduction in or avoidance of alcohol and caffeine. These are not magical solutions — no one has ever survived emotionally traumatic times simply by ceasing to drink coffee. But such actions can be simple ways to take control of part of your life, to reduce some amount of stress-related symptoms, and to promote a sense of physical well-being.

Learn to Relax

In the early days of psychosomatic medicine, it was commonplace for patients to complain to their family physicians about noticeable physical symptoms, only to be told, "It's just stress," or "It's all in your mind." As a result, many people left the doctor feeling misunderstood or that they were crazy or just imagining these problems.

Emotional distress is more than just a state of mind; it's much more than just feeling bad or having negative, unpleasant thoughts. During times of emotional stress, bona fide physical changes and symptoms do occur, some of which are uncomfortable and painful and some of which can actually lead to life-threatening illnesses. There is clear evidence to suggest that significant stress, including anxiety and depression, can lead to profound changes in brain chemistry, including the release of many different hormones from the endocrine glands of the body (the pituitary gland, the adrenal gland and the thyroid gland).

Hormones are specifically designed to regulate normal metabolic functioning, controlling or influencing many basic biological rhythms, drives and processes. Without the combined effort of intricately complex hormone systems, survival would be impossible. However, during times of stress the brain can activate the endocrine system in a way that results in such stress-related physical symptoms as rapid heart rate, high blood pressure, decreases or increases in metabolic activity. In addition, the hormone system can profoundly affect the functioning of the immune system, altering the functioning of specific white blood cells.

The ultimate solution to reducing stress is to come to terms with painful life events or to alter the course of those events in your life. In the short run, you can employ a number of strategies to reduce physical distress. Relaxation exercises (sometimes accompanied by biofeedback) and meditative techniques are widely used as treatments (or adjunct treatments) for many physical illnesses, including migraine headaches, hypertension, ulcers, chronic pain conditions, chronic fatigue syndrome, and others.

> *The ultimate solution to reducing stress is to come to terms with painful life events...*

It is common to give some "good advice" to friends who are under stress: "just relax." We're not talking about "just relaxing" here, but offering specific procedures that have been demonstrated to have a profound effect on physical functioning. The techniques described on pages 72 - 73 are two effective proven procedures for learning to relax deeply.

You'll have to discover for yourself whether the *progressive muscle relaxation* technique or *visualization* (or a combination of the two) works best. Please keep in mind that simple relaxation techniques obviously don't solve major life crises. "Just relaxing" or "taking it easy" are not the answers as we go through difficult times. (We want to emphasize also that the specific procedures described here are of proven value — hundreds of careful studies have shown their effectiveness. Sitting in front of the TV with a beer — or even vacationing in Hawaii — may sound easier and perhaps more appealing, but those activities are not particularly helpful in countering stress over the long haul.)

Relaxation Techniques

Two common and effective techniques have been found to be especially helpful ways to learn to relax completely: progressive muscle relaxation and visualization.

Progressive Muscle Relaxation. During times of stress, particular muscles and muscle groups tend automatically to become tense. Progressive muscle relaxation techniques are designed to reduce tension in all the body's muscle groups.

The relaxation procedure requires a period of time when you will not be disturbed. Sit in a comfortable chair, or recline on a couch or on a carpeted floor. Close your eyes and take two slow, deep breaths. As you exhale slowly, notice the gradual release of tension in chest and shoulder muscles. Feel the weight of your body against the chair (couch, floor), and the gentle pull of gravity as you settle into the chair. After a few moments, you can begin a series of simple exercises, tensing particular muscles, holding the tension for a count of "three" and then releasing. Each time you tense and then release, you can enhance the effect by paying special attention to the experience of relaxation/letting-go that occurs immediately after release.

Allow ten or fifteen seconds between each tensing of muscles before proceeding to the next muscle group. The tensing exercises begin with the feet and progress like this:

1. Feet/toes
2. Calves/lower legs
3. Thighs
4. Buttocks (squeeze together)
5. Abdomen
6. Lower back (arch)
7. Chest (hold in a deep breath)
8. Hands (make fists)
9. Upper arms
10. Shoulders (shrug)
11. Face (squeeze eyes and mouth closed)
12. Face (open eyes and mouth)

Many experts on relaxation techniques recommend fifteen to twenty minutes twice a day to go through this exercise, especially when you're first learning the procedure. It's been our experience, however, that few people will find time to do this on a regular basis. A realistic alternative, after you've practiced for a week or so and learned how to relax deeply, is to abbreviate the technique by omitting the tensing step and simply relaxing each muscle group in turn. This whole procedure can easily be done in two to three minutes, and repeated several times a day. When time allows, you can, of course, give yourself permission to expand the procedure and achieve an even deeper sense of relaxation.

You'll notice immediately a significant reduction of muscular tension. More important, if the exercise is done several times a day (even briefly) on a regular basis, it can reduce *chronic* tension levels. You may notice less daytime fatigue, more productive energy, and an improved ability to fall asleep.

Visualization. Many different visualization techniques have been developed. Here's a description of one of the most commonly employed:

Begin by finding a quiet time and a comfortable chair or couch. Close your eyes and take two slow, deep breaths. Notice the physical sensations of relaxation as you gently exhale.

After a few moments, imagine yourself standing at the top of a flight of stairs with ten steps. In a moment you can begin to see yourself slowly and gradually walking down the stairs, one at a time. When you begin your descent, you will notice a sense of increasing relaxation as you move downward. With each step, experience the feeling of deeper and deeper relaxation. As you take each step, silently count to yourself: ten... and nine... and eight... lower and lower as you go. Throughout your descent, you feel safe and in control, as you choose to let go of tension. The mental image of downward movement has been found to trigger a relaxation response.

As you reach the bottom of the stairs — and two...and one — let your mind take you to a particular setting, a place you know that you associate with feelings of comfort, security and well-being. It may be a beautiful meadow, a warm, sunny beach, or a rustic cabin in the forest. The choice is yours as you create your own personal image of serenity. The experience of relaxation is enhanced by taking particular note of all sensory experiences in your image (the sights, sounds, smells, and feelings of the peaceful setting).

After a few minutes, you can decide to leave the relaxing setting by slowly counting from three to one — three... and two... and one — as your eyes open and you again are fully alert, but relaxed.

Progressive muscle relaxation and visualization clearly do reduce physical tension, and they are ways that you can give yourself some amount of self-nurturing. They are direct ways to exert some control over tension while taking other actions to promote coping and emotional healing. (For a more complete discussion, please see books by Davis, et al., and Benson, listed in the References.)

Your therapist can assist you with these procedures, if you need additional help, or she/he may have other suggestions to add to your repertoire of tools for dealing with physical and emotional stress. You can't have too many!

16: Doing "Homework" That Heals

There are several easy things you can do between sessions that can help a lot to speed up the process of therapy. It's a kind of "homework" — but you won't be graded. These simple strategies have been developed, tested out and found quite helpful for people going through a wide array of difficult times. Let's take a look at six specific "homework" strategies.

What Works and What Doesn't

Often during times of stress, people conclude "Nothing I do seems to help." Most times this statement is only partially true.

Jim and Mary come to a brief therapy session and continue to talk about marital problems. They just told the therapist that "We had a bad week." The therapist listened to the details, and at some point asked, "Were there any good times during the past week?" The couple said "Yes... Saturday was pretty good."

You can look at this kind of situation and simply think, "Well, it was nice to have at least one good day"...and then, just forget about it. An alternative however, is to think, *"Why* was it good day? Could I have *two* good days next week?"

The therapist encouraged Jim and Mary to think carefully about Saturday, and to try to discover any clues to why things went well. Mary said, "Saturday, Jim saw that I was pretty overwhelmed with the kids and he came up to me and said, 'Let me help out'... That was kinda unique for him to say something like this, and I think it set the tone for the whole day. I really appreciated it."

When Jim confirmed the story, the therapist said, "I have a suggestion. We've focused a lot on problems and what doesn't work. But you've just told me that there really are times when the two of you can have a good day. I think it would be helpful to start paying attention to the good times. When you feel good about each other or you feel close, sit down and think, 'What made this possible?... What did I say or do, what did she say or do that really made a difference?' And write it down in a notebook. I know there are some serious problems in your relationship, but there may be some solutions there too. Your homework assignment is to start noting those more positive times and start keeping a notebook — jotting down 'things that help' and 'things that work.' I think it'll help. Are you willing to give it a try?"

Many people discover to their surprise that there already are some things they do that succeed in reducing distress or minimizing conflicts. These are strengths you can build on!

Psychiatrist Gordon Deckert also suggests a simple and straightforward idea. When you keep trying to deal with a recurring problem in a particular way, and it doesn't work, stop and take a close look at what you're doing (that doesn't work) and at the very least, just don't do *that!* Most of us are creatures of habit and it's normal to do things in the "usual way" — even when the evidence is abundant that it doesn't work!

Mike gives us another example. Whenever he had a frustrating week he'd feel depressed, discouraged and rather hopeless. His usual solution was to shut himself away in his apartment all weekend... not going outside and not having contact with others. His therapist asked him if this "solution" was helpful. Mike replied, "I don't feel like doing anything but hiding out at home all weekend, but I guess it doesn't help much... By Sunday night I usually feel worse."

His therapist inquired, "Have there ever been times when you were feeling down, but you *didn't* lock yourself away in your apartment?" Mike answered, "Yes... on occasion." He went on to elaborate how on these rare occasions he didn't *feel* like going out, but he forced himself to leave his apartment and go to the mall, or to the park, or bowling with a friend. And most times it helped him feel somewhat better.

The best way to approach this is to look carefully at what you do when times are difficult (maybe even write it down on paper) and then ask yourself, "Does this help me? Is it a good solution?" Some solutions aren't chosen; they feel automatic. And some solutions backfire; they either don't help or even make things feel worse. You do have choices. Take action! Even if you can't invent a great solution, at least stop doing things that don't work.

Sixty-Second Reality Check

Especially during times of stress it's common to experience moments of very strong, upsetting feelings. One form of "homework" that just takes a minute is what we call the *60-second reality check*. This is a simple but powerful technique that can often help you gain perspective and reduce distress in just a minute. Here's how it works: As soon as something has happened that has triggered a very strong feeling (e.g., irritation), take just a moment to go through the following list:

1. Does this (what's just happened) really matter to me?
2. In the grand scheme of things, how big a deal is it?
    Is it a true catastrophe?
    Is it likely to seem like a big deal in 24 hours?
    Is it likely to seem like a big deal in one week?
3. Am I taking it personally?

4. If I react now will it:
      Probably be helpful?
      Probably make things worse?
5. Would it make sense to take time to think through the situation and then decide how to react?
6. Are my thoughts and actions helping me or hurting me? What I'm thinking or telling myself right now — is it helpful or is it hurtful?

It is important to emphasize that this technique is *not* designed to help you talk yourself out of feeling the way you do. It's very important to be true to how you really feel. At the same time, reflect a bit on how you really see a situation, so that you may then choose wisely how you want to respond. This brief "reality check" is a good way to gain perspective quickly and avoid impulsive reactions.

Turning Down the Volume on Strong Feelings

The intention here is *not* to deny or minimize real, honest feelings, but rather to do something that can help you feel in *control* of your emotions. People often say or think certain words and phrases that operate like emotion amplifiers. Often, simply rephrasing (or reframing) your thoughts and words de-intensifies emotions without negating how you truly feel. Here is a very brief list of rephrases that you may find helpful.

You Say or Think	Rephrased
I really need it!	It's not that I absolutely *need* it... rather, I really *want* it
I feel guilty and am a bad person	I am not a bad person, but I do feel regret
It shouldn't be that way	It is and I don't like it
I'm being too sensitive	I do have strong feelings about this
It's a catastrophe	It's important and it matters a lot... although it may not be a complete catastrophe

Positive Activity Diary

Annie is a thirty-five-year-old woman who came to brief therapy complaining of depression: "I can't get anything accomplished. I'm at home all day with the kids. By the time my husband gets home, the house is a wreck. I look at my house and think, 'What's wrong with me?' I don't even work. I'm just a housewife and I can't get anything done. I feel out of control of my whole life!" She considered herself an inadequate mother and housekeeper, who "does nothing productive." Since Annie has three children, ages one, two and four, it was hard for her therapist to believe her statements, "I don't even work," and "I can't get anything done."

The therapist asked Annie to start keeping an *activity diary*, at least for one day. He asked her to write down *everything* she did, even small things like picking up a toy or getting a drink for one of her children. She brought to the next session a small notebook with many pages filled. She said, "I can't believe it. As I was writing everything down, it hit me. I'm continuously busy from morning 'til night. In fact, it was hard to keep up with the writing... I know I missed some things. Maybe my house looks like a wreck, but at least I know that I'm working my butt off. I *am* getting a lot done each day."

Especially if you feel overwhelmed or depressed, it's easy to overlook or minimize your accomplishments. At the end of the day you may conclude, "The day was wasted. I got nothing done." This perception lowers self-esteem and brings a sense of defeat. An activity diary can help present a more realistic view of events.

There are two ways you can do this. First, *write down every single activity,* as Annie tried to do. This does take some time and is not practical for most of us on a regular basis. Still, doing it for a day or two can be helpful, as it was for Annie. A more practical approach for use on a daily basis is to *record the major events* of each day: *tasks completed* (or progress made towards completion); *positive events,* (receiving a compliment, pampering yourself with a hot bubble bath, having a nice lunch with a friend, getting a letter, feeling good about a job well done); and *experiences* that matter to you (spending time with your child, gardening, writing a letter to a friend, saying a prayer.)

This process works best if you keep it simple and easy. It is best to jot down only very brief three- to five-word statements. Then, review the list at the end of the day. Even very distressed people who feel as though they accomplished absolutely nothing in a day are often surprised to find out that in fact they've done many things and experienced some moments of pleasure. This approach is very easy to put into action and can give immediate pay-offs. It's an important way to avoid feelings of helplessness and low self-esteem.

Mood-Rating Chart

People who are under tremendous stress commonly look back over a period of time and remember primarily the negative feelings and events. They tend to conclude, "I've had an awful week. Everything went wrong. The whole week was terrible." This type of memory (which accentuates unpleasant experiences) can actually make stress worse. Believing that nothing positive happens in your life, or that you are always extremely depressed, can result in increased feelings of despair and pessimism. The fact is that *even very stressed people are not 100 percent distressed all of the time.* Even during very hard times people experience ups and downs. A person's mood is almost never completely stable. It is important and helpful to have an accurate and realistic perception of one's moods and to be able to monitor changes in mood over time. An effective way to accomplish this is to use a *daily mood rating chart*. A number of studies have demonstrated that simply tracking and rating one's moods on a daily basis has the effect of deceasing stress. At first glance this might seem absurd, but let's look at this approach and understand how keeping track can help.

The use of a mood rating chart is simple. Take a look at the sample chart, page 80. (Feel free to make copies of this chart for your personal use.) Place a copy of the chart on your bedside table, and each night take a few moments to review the day. Ask yourself:

Mood Rating:															Days:
-7	-6	-5	-4	-3	-2	-1	0	+1	+2	+3	+4	+5	+6	+7	
															1
															2
															3
															4
															5
															6
															7
															8
															9
															10
															11
															12
															13
															14
															15
															16
															17
															18
															19
															20
															21
															22
															23
															24
															25
															26
															27
															28

+7 Best day of my life

0 Neutral

-7 Absolutely worst day of my life

DAILY MOOD RATING CHART   Starting Date: _____

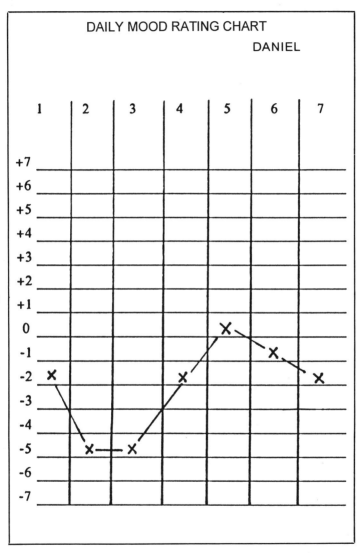

"Overall, how did I feel today?" and then rate your feelings on a scale of from plus 7 (extremely happy day) to minus 7 (extremely unhappy day). Most people will notice that there is a good deal of change in mood from day to day.

Daniel is a forty-two-year-old college professor who has been experiencing painful depressive symptoms since his wife asked him for a divorce a month ago. During his first therapy session he said, "Every single day, I feel paralyzed with depression. I have no energy, no motivation and no happiness." During the next week he completed a daily mood rating chart and brought it in to the next session (please see page 81). In looking at this chart, he commented, "There were several days when I felt extremely depressed, but now looking back over the week, there were a couple of days that were not terrible, and most of the time I was not at rock bottom." This chart was helpful for him in two ways. First, it helped him remember more accurately and realistically how he was feeling. He soon realized that his depression, while certainly a painful experience, was not 100 percent pervasive. This acknowledgement helped to inspire hope, and left him feeling not quite so powerless. Secondly, he was able to use the chart over a period of two months to monitor his recovery from depression. After eight weeks of therapy, he said, "I've been noticing that gradually, over the past weeks, more and more of my days are good days. I still get discouraged and have some crummy days, but there definitely is a positive trend. I am feeling better."

Keeping Perspective

Another homework project you may find helpful is to make a list of "things that matter." In the midst of hard times, it's easy to focus mainly on bad stuff, and to lose sight of positive aspects of life. Our college professor, Daniel, made the following list:

Things That Matter To Me

1. My relationship with my kids.
2. My teaching job and how I have an impact on my students.
3. My involvement in church and our fund-raising activities.
4. Reading exciting novels.
5. Listening to rock and roll music.
6. Sailing.
7. Exercising at the Y.
8. Talking to my sister on the phone.
9. Writing to or calling old friends.
10. Driving in the country on a sunny weekend afternoon.
11. The fact that I am a decent person and a good father.
12. My sense of humor.

Daniel wrote this list on a piece of paper, taped it to his bathroom mirror, and on the bottom in red ink wrote: "Dan — Don't forget these things. They are important!" His divorce was very tough and many days were filled with sadness. But keeping in touch with positive things about himself and remembering to notice those things that matter helped him make it through even really hard days.

The homework activities in this chapter can be of particular value if you review them with your therapist throughout the course of your brief therapy. The ideas are flexible. Work with your therapist to adapt them to your needs so they will contribute most to your emotional healing.

17: Strengthening Your "Self"

Citizens in coastal regions of the Southeastern U.S. occasionally must prepare for the onslaught of a hurricane. With a day or two of warning, people in their communities place boards on windows, tie down trees and secure other possessions, bracing for the storm. No amount of human action can lessen the force of the hurricane winds, but the preparation can make a significant difference in how well people weather the storm.

Similarly, during times of emotional crisis people can take steps to ride out emotional storms more successfully. These actions, we believe, have one thing in common: they strengthen a person's *sense of self*.

Underdeveloped Sense of Self

- You're easily manipulated by others.
- In the presence of powerful others, you lose sight of how you really feel and what you really want. Readily changing your needs and opinions to please others.
- You're unclear about your own preferences and priorities.
- You often act out of compliance or an over-readiness to compromise or please others.
- You're unable to clearly define and pursue important life activities (job, hobbies, social causes).
- You are living your life for others, not out of your own unique, inner self.
- You easily lose your good mood if you encounter someone who is depressed or irritated.

A More Solidly Developed Sense of Self[1]

- You trust your own values, beliefs, and feelings.
- You believe you are the only person who really knows you.
- You're reasonably clear about how you really feel and what you truly want.
- You're able to make clear statements to others, expressing emotions, beliefs and making requests.
- You're able to maintain your relationships with others in difficult times.
- You're able to take positions on things that matter.
- You live by your own personal values, beliefs and limits.
- You're able to acknowledge and benefit from your strengths and your weaknesses.
- You trust your intuitions, hunches and "gut feelings."
- You have compassion for yourself (without feeling guilty).

[1]A number of these are drawn from *Dance of Intimacy,* a highly recommended book by Harriet Goldhar Lerner.

But what exactly is this notion of *sense of self?* Maybe it can best be described by giving examples of an underdeveloped sense of self and in contrast, a more solidly developed sense of self. (See list on page 84.)

A childhood in which a person is truly loved, valued, and nurtured is the foundation for a solid sense of self. Yet many, many people did not have an idyllic childhood; for lots of us, growing up was difficult (sometimes extremely difficult). Fortunately, there are a number of things you can do to discover and strengthen your sense of self. Regardless of the emotional stresses you may be encountering, you can likely benefit from the suggestions that follow.

"I yam what I yam." — Popeye

One of the most emotionally damaging experiences a person can encounter is *invalidation.* Many of us have been told (in one way or another) "You *shouldn't* be so emotional," "You *should* stop acting so childish," "You *should* be ashamed of yourself," "Who the hell do you think you are?!"

You are who you are. Yet all of us are sometimes greeted with such statements of criticism, shame and invalidation. The message that comes through is, "Who you are (how you act or feel) is *not okay.* You should be *ashamed.*" These reactions from others have a powerful impact on the self, especially in childhood. In the wake of shaming and critical comment, many young people turn inward, grit their teeth, ignore inner feelings and comply. The *true self* is stifled, and may remain underdeveloped.

Conversely, acceptance, validation and affirmation from others act powerfully to relieve suffering. To feel accepted, to feel believed, to have others understand — all these provide tremendous emotional support at times of despair, helping us to recognize and develop our own "true selves."

One of the reasons therapy can be of such value is that good therapists provide acceptance, belief and understanding — validation of who you are. Validation, however, comes not only from others, but also from within yourself. A crucial aspect of strengthening your "self" is to *allow yourself to believe your inner experiences.* Many people may think, "I shouldn't feel this way," or "I'm making mountains out of mole hills," when the simple truth is that they hurt. Self-validation is *acknowledging* your inner feelings and *accepting* them as real and understandable. It certainly does not mean that in any way you *like* the experience, that you choose to wallow in the pain, or that you accept the pain as your "lot in life." It is merely an open and honest acknowledgement of your emotional reality. Awareness and acknowledgement of inner truths can serve as an anchor during hard times. "I yam what I yam."

Speak Up!

A second step to take in strengthening your sense of self is to find outlets for *honest self-expression.* Weak muscles can gradually become strengthened by exercising. Self-expression is the type of emotional exercise that gradually builds and strengthens the self. Another major benefit of psychotherapy comes from your ability to clarify your inner feelings, needs, and beliefs and to voice these out loud with your therapist. This single experience can leave you feeling more real and more solid about yourself.

Honest self-expression also means open verbal communication with others in your life: assertively expressing your opinions, beliefs, values, needs, taking a stand, saying "no," asking for change in others' behavior (see Chapter 14).

Keep Track

Many people have found tremendous value in keeping a *personal journal.* Writing down feelings, thoughts, hopes and dreams can be a powerful way to clarify inner emotional experiences and find an outlet for self-expression.

Take Care of Yourself

The self always flourishes best in a healthy atmosphere, which you can create by giving yourself permission to *care for basic physical and emotional needs*: adequate rest, good nutrition, exercise, fresh air; surrounding yourself with things of beauty; making a place in your home that can be a haven of warmth, comfort and peace; making time for recreation, humor, relaxation, or meditation; establishing a reasonable balance between work and play; setting realistic expectations for yourself; and, from time to time, splurging. All of these sound incredibly simple and obvious, but these issues often go unnoticed (even by psychologists who write self-help books) and can contribute to an underlying sense of dis-ease. Some people may think these ideas sound selfish. If so, it's a smart kind of selfishness since it helps people feel better, more alive, and in the long run, ultimately affects the lives of others in a positive way, too. (Take another look at Chapter 14, also.)

Get Involved

Finally, and as important as any of the ideas in this chapter, you may strengthen your sense of self by *becoming involved in life activities* that express and affirm your own inner beliefs and values. You may accomplish this through your choice of career. Many people realize this goal through involvement in churches, organizations and causes that have personal meaning. Dozens of volunteer agencies and support programs in every community offer hundreds of opportunities for each of us to give something back to the world. Not only can these activities help the community, but they also can become an important vehicle for your own self-expression. Making a positive contribution to others — connecting with the world beyond yourself — is arguably the best way to begin to feel better about yourself.

Your journey through difficult times — with or without therapy — is easier when you feel a more solid sense of yourself.

PART IV
Are Medications The Answer?

18: A Brief Guide To
Psychiatric Medications

These days you don't have to be seriously mentally ill to be prescribed psychiatric medications. In mental health clinics across the country, millions of people are being helped by brief therapy and also benefiting from the appropriate use of certain psychiatric medications. Let's see what this is all about.

Research, especially during the past decade, has made it clear that the symptoms of *some* major mental disorders are related to chemical changes in the brain. Examples: psychotic disorders, panic disorder, depression, manic depressive illness, attention deficit disorder. As millions of people can attest, gritting your teeth, trying harder or using will power simply doesn't work to overcome these painful symptoms.

Renowned psychiatrist Dr. Karl Menninger is credited with the observation that medications will probably never be developed which can fill empty lives or mend broken hearts. There is no kind of medication that can give a person a sense of connection with other human beings, a feeling of self, or the kind of values that make life worth living. At the same time, many newly developed psychotropic medications can dramatically affect the course of a person's life in a positive sense, and can help some people achieve much better outcomes in brief therapy.

Be an Informed Consumer

Many people do not need medications; on the other hand, many folks are helped tremendously from this type of treatment. We want you to be well informed about the role of medication in brief therapy so you can make decisions about the possible use of psychiatric medications in your own treatment.

In the past, patients were given prescriptions by the doctor and simply told, "Take these and call me if you don't get better." These days, everyone is more sophisticated. Today's patients want and need to know about what to expect from medication treatment, the risks and benefits, the possible side effects. In our view, this a healthy development. Rather than being a "passive patient," it makes more sense to be actively involved in your treatment, to be knowledgeable, to ask questions, and to collaborate with your doctor as you work together to solve problems.

In this chapter, we'll give you the basics about psychiatric medications, so you can ask your doctor good questions about any and all concerns you may have about pursuing this aspect of treatment. When used appropriately, psychiatric medications can make an enormous difference in reducing some types of human misery.

Psychiatric medications don't treat all forms of emotional pain, of course. We'll focus here on those particular disorders that respond well to drug treatment, beginning with anxiety and depression, the most commonly encountered emotional problems.

Depression

Many people suffer from mild bouts of depression that may last a few days to a few weeks. However more serious forms of depression can last for months or years unless properly treated. Three types of depression have been shown to respond well to antidepressant medication treatment:

• **Major Depression:** Moderate to severe depression that may last for many months, if not treated. Antidepressant medications can be effective in 80%+ of cases of major depression. This is especially true if any of the following symptoms are present (these are symptoms therapists look for to determine if medication treatment is warranted):

- Extreme sadness, despair or irritability
- Unusual sleep habits: Severe insomnia or excessive sleeping
- Pronounced fatigue
- Appetite changes (with either weight gain *or* weight loss)
- Loss of sex drive
- An inability to experience joy or pleasure
- Strong suicidal ideas.

• **Dysthymia:** This very long-term, low-grade depression often begins in adolescence and may last a lifetime. Studies have shown that about 55% of people who suffer from dysthymia have a good response to antidepressants. The symptoms include:

- Negative, pessimistic thinking
- Low self-esteem; feelings of inadequacy
- Low energy and fatigue
- Lack of motivation and enthusiasm
- A decreased zest for life.

• **Bi-Polar (Manic-Depressive) Disorder:** This is a very serious psychiatric condition that causes extreme mood swings, from severe depression to episodes of mania (extra-high energy, agitation, decreased need for sleep, rapid speech, racing thoughts). All people with suspected bipolar disorder *must* be evaluated by a psychiatrist, and the disorder *must be treated with medications* (generally antidepressants and a mood stabilizer such as lithium). Without medical treatment, people with bipolar disorder typically become progressively worse, and this grave disorder has a very high suicide rate.

• **Antidepressant Medications:** Many forms of depression involve a biochemical malfunction in the brain. Antidepressants are a class of medications which have been shown to be highly effective in reducing a number of depressive symptoms. It is important to note the following:

♦ Antidepressants are *not* tranquilizers. *Unless anxiety is a major component, tranquilizers are* not *an appropriate treatment for depression.*

♦ Antidepressants are *not* addictive.

♦ When prescribed they *must* be taken every day (as prescribed) if they are to work.

♦ When taking antidepressants patients are advised not to drink alcoholic beverages, since alcohol interferes with the effectiveness of the drug.

♦ Antidepressants (unfortunately) do not work overnight. It typically takes two to four weeks to notice the first signs of improvement. It's essential to know this so you won't feel discouraged during the first couple of weeks.

♦ If one antidepressant medication does not work, there are many other options. Most people can be successfully treated, although sometimes two or three medications must be tried in order to find the right drug for the patient's unique biochemical and emotional needs.

♦ Once symptoms have significantly improved, it is very important to continue taking the medication for at least six months to avoid relapse.

♦ Antidepressants are not "happy pills." They simply operate to restore normal biological functioning (e.g., improved sleep, appetite and energy levels).

♦ Antidepressants restore normal chemical functioning in the brain (much like insulin helps diabetics function normally). Thus, this treatment should not be seen as a "chemical crutch," but rather a medical treatment that effectively returns one to normal biologic functioning.

♦ Side effects of antidepressants are generally mild and not dangerous. Side effects vary depending on what medication is used, but may include drowsiness, dry mouth and mild nausea. Ask your physician/ psychiatrist for a list of specific side effects that may occur with the particular medication prescribed for you.

Antidepressant Medications

Generic	Brand
imipramine	Tofranil
desipramine	Norpramin
amitriptyline	Elavil
nortriptyline	Aventyl
nortriptyline	Pamelor
protriptyline	Vivactil
trimipramine	Surmontil
doxepin	Sinequan
doxepin	Adapin
maprotiline	Ludiomil
amoxapine	Asendin
trazodone	Desyrel
fluoxetine	Prozac
bupropion	Wellbutrin
sertraline	Zoloft
paroxetine	Paxil
venlafaxine	Effexor
nefazodone	Serzone
MAO Inhibitors	
phenelzine	Nardil
tranylcypromine	Parnate

Anxiety and Panic

Not all types of anxiety are effectively treated by medication, however, two types of anxiety disorders have been shown to respond well:

• **Panic Disorder:** This disorder is characterized by brief episodes of intense panic that come on very suddenly and usually last for only a few minutes (typically 1-20 minutes). During an attack, a person may experience the following symptoms:

    ♦ Trembling, nervousness, panic

    ♦ Shortness of breath and a smothering sensation

    ♦ Rapid heart beat, lightheadedness, dizziness

♦ A fear of impending doom (often the belief that "I'm going to die" or "I'm going crazy.")

Panic is a terribly unpleasant disorder that, thankfully, is very treatable with certain psychiatric medications.

• **Anti-Panic Medications:** Psychotropic drugs used to treat panic include two options:

♦ *Antidepressants* (see chart, page 92) All antidepressants have been shown to effectively treat panic disorder with one exception, the drug bupropion. All of the statements made earlier regarding antidepressant treatment also apply to the treatment of panic attacks. It must be emphasized that antidepressants must be taken on a daily basis and it generally requires 2-3 weeks of treatment before panic symptoms begin to diminish.

♦ *High Potency Tranquilizers*: The tranquilizers alprazolam (Xanax) and clonazepam (Klonopin) are fast acting medications that are quite effective in treating panic disorder. Often panic attacks can be reduced or eliminated within a few days of starting treatment with these medications. However, tranquilizers have three major problems. The first is drowsiness. The second is that they should never be discontinued abruptly. Finally, tranquilizers can become drugs of abuse. However, this typically only occurs in people who have a history of prior drug or alcohol abuse (or people who have a lot of biological relatives with drug and alcohol abuse problems). Generally in these cases, tranquilizers should not be used.

It makes sense to actively be involved in your treatment, to be knowledgeable, to ask questions, and to collaborate with your doctor as you work together to solve problems.

Psychiatrists often find a combination of antidepressant and tranquilizer quite successful.

The majority of people suffering from panic disorder must take medications for at least one year, often longer.

• **Severe Anxiety Following Major Life Crises:** Short-term use of tranquilizers (in addition to brief therapy) is sometimes recommended in the wake of serious life crises. The medications are used (often for only a couple of weeks) to target two main symptoms: insomnia (especially difficulty falling asleep), and *nervousness and restlessness.* A list of commonly used tranquilizers follows:

Antianxiety Medications

Generic	Brand
for nervousness	
buspirone	BuSpar
chlordiazepoxide	Librium
oxazepam	Serax
clorazepate	Tranxene
lorazepam	Ativan
prazepam	Centrax
alprazolam	Xanax
clonazepam	Klonopin
for insomnia	
flurazepam	Dalmane
temazepam	Restoril
triazolam	Halcion
quazepam	Doral
zolpidem	Ambien
estazolam	Prosom

♦ As with antidepressants, patients should not drink alcohol when taking these medications.

♦ These should not be used in individuals with a drug or alcohol abuse history (except the drug buspirone).

♦ Never discontinue treatment abruptly. Always check with your physician before stopping treatment.

Other Disorders

We've focussed primarily on the treatment of anxiety and depression in this chapter. Other emotional and psychiatric disorders can be successfully treated with psychiatric medications, however *typically not within the context of brief therapy.* In this section we will briefly list the symptoms of several disorders and medication options. Please refer to the books noted in the References section for details on drug treatment for various psychiatric disorders.

• **Obsessive-Compulsive Disorder:** Recurring, persistent unpleasant or senseless thoughts or impulses which are difficult to prevent or ignore. Behavior includes repetitive actions or rituals carried out in an attempt to reduce obsessive ideas (e.g., repeatedly checking to see if doors and windows are locked; repeatedly washing hands).

Medication Options:

Generic	Brand
clomipramine	Anafranil
fluoxetine	Prozac
sertraline	Zoloft
paroxetine	Paxil
fluvoxamine	Luvox

• **Bulimia:** Binge eating followed by: self-induced vomiting, laxative use, strict dieting or excessive exercise to prevent weight gain.

Medication Options: Antidepressants

• **Psychotic Disorders** (including schizophrenia, some forms of bipolar disorder and paranoia). These very serious forms of mental illness have such symptoms as:
  • Hallucinations, bizarre or unrealistic thoughts
  • Confusion and grossly impaired judgement
  • Agitation or chaotic behavior.

Medication Options: Antipsychotic medications, such as chlorpromazine (Thorazine) or haloperidol (Haldol).

- **Post-Traumatic Stress Disorder (PTSD):** This disorder often includes a rather characteristic group of symptoms in response to exposure to life events that were either extremely dangerous or frightening and/or in which a person encountered a tremendous sense of powerlessness. The event may be a recent trauma or may be an event that occurred many years earlier. (In the latter case, a person may massively block out the memory and feelings of the original event(s), which begin to surface months or years later in the form of intrusive memories or dreams.)

Symptoms of PTSD include:

- Vivid re-experiencing of the traumatic event in thoughts, recollections or nightmares
- Avoiding situations which remind one of the traumatic event
- Memory impairment (e.g., amnesia for the event)
- Feelings of numbness, detachment and unreality
- Intense feelings of anxiety, irritability or depression

Medication Options: Antidepressants; some tranquilizers

You're Calling the Shots

As an informed consumer and collaborator in your own medication treatment, remember — you're calling the shots. It's *your choice* whether or not to take psychotropic medication. *You* know how you respond to the treatment (positive effects and, at times, side effects). Discuss freely with your therapist any concerns you have about this part of treatment.

PART V. Managing Under Managed Care

19: Finding Your Way Through the Managed Care Maze

Brief therapy has been around for many years, in one form or another. Why is it suddenly so popular? The answers are simple — and incredibly complex — *time* and *money.*

Everyone feels the press of time these days. We all want to deal with problems quickly and get on with our lives. Brief therapy can't solve all the problems we face but, as you've seen in this book, it can be a great help. That makes brief therapy a very attractive option.

"Brief" is also generally seen as "cost effective." With health care costs escalating out of sight, procedures that provide effective treatment at low cost are in great demand. Private and government health insurance programs and health care organizations have looked for every possible way to cut costs, and "cost effective" has become a mantra repeated by regulators, health professionals, and patients alike.

The system that evolved in response to these demands has come to be known as "managed care." For better or for worse, the "managers" are the outfits that pay the bills — insurance companies, government agencies, health maintenance organizations.

With the advent of managed care, health care as many of us have known it is forever changed. The "good old days" of the 1960s, '70s and '80s — when you could see any physician or health care provider and have your insurance pick up the tab — are long gone for most of us.

And you're not exempt from some of these changes if you use a public hospital or university counseling center, or even if you pay for your own health care. The new system has changed more than just the way the bills are paid. The pace of everything is faster now, and all benefits are subject to careful evaluation and review. Doctors don't have much time to "visit" with patients anymore. Health care — including psychotherapy — follows a briefer problem-solving model more than ever before.

In the mental health field, the new brief care standards have become routine in independent and group private practice, community mental health centers, college and university counseling centers and health clinics, public and private hospital psychiatry departments... virtually anywhere mental health professionals practice.

For simplicity in this chapter, we'll discuss all brief therapy settings as "managed care," although university centers and other public agencies may not use that term. There will, of course, be differences among the various agencies, but the processes of intake, referral, planning and evaluation — and the headaches of paperwork — are similar.

> *Keep in mind that the discussion in this chapter refers to programs of therapy that are covered as benefits under a health care plan. You can get virtually any therapy you want or need if you are able and willing to pay for it yourself.*

What Mental Health Benefits are Available Under Managed Care?

Most managed care companies and agencies offer restricted mental health benefits. You can't just pick up a phone book and choose a doctor or counselor. And you can't get coverage for all conditions. Getting what you need under managed care is rarely as simple as the ads for your care plan would have you believe!

To ensure you have as much information as possible and can make educated choices as a proactive, responsible partner in obtaining your own care, read your benefits book *carefully* and *completely,* until you understand it. Ask questions. Don't be afraid to advocate for what you want, to ask questions about your benefits or about services that seem to be missing or about how to obtain *any* particular benefit. Most managed care organizations are willing to spend time with you on the phone to help you understand what services you are eligible for and how to access them.

Typical mental health conditions covered under managed care tend to be those that require an *immediate* intervention:

- *Emergency care* — for patients who may be dangerous to themselves or others.
- *Acute care* — for short-term life crises.
- *Marital or family conflict* — especially if abuse is involved.
- *Brief solution-focused problem solving.*
- *Assessment and referral for chronic mental illness* — screening for long-term therapy.

How Can You Make Managed Care Work for You?

For you, as a consumer and client, the easiest, most useful way to get services is to educate yourself regarding several basic aspects and limitations of the managed care model.

When you want or need to seek emotional support under your health care plan, remember that there is almost always a "protocol" to follow — a specific set of predictable steps and tasks you *must* follow in order to get services.

Often the mental health benefit (or "behavioral health" benefit as it is often called) requires a referral from your "primary care" physician. Thus, under the managed care plan, you can no longer simply see *any* licensed mental health professional, but must first request this service from your insurance plan, directly or through your primary care physician. The primary care provider is often (but not always) a general or family practitioner who has been assigned primary responsibility for your health care. In most plans, any referral to a needed specialist — including a psychotherapist — must come from your primary care provider. (In *some* plans, e.g., Kaiser, student counseling centers — a referral from a physician is not required.)

The thinking behind this "gatekeeper" approach is that by paying a general or family practitioner to handle most aspects of your care, the funding agency has a better handle on your actual medical needs.[1]

Help At Last!

When you get your referral it will often be directly to either a Department of Psychiatry (if you belong to a "staff" based model like Kaiser-Permanente), or to a specific person or group (if you belong to a "panel" based model like Champus — a "panel" is a list of independent providers and practice groups who are approved by the plan). Most referrals are for a limited number of sessions, encouraging psychotherapists who work in managed care to adopt a brief therapy model.

Your therapist's first job, regardless of the model used as the basis of providing treatment, is to understand and assess as quickly as possible what is troubling you and how best to treat it. Based upon the initial assessment, the therapist will develop a "treatment plan" designed to assist you. In managed care, the treatment plan is based on resolving your current condition within the limits of your health benefits plan. After the number of therapy sessions called for in the treatment plan, additional sessions must be authorized through the managed care system's review process, and will be allowed *only* if need is shown. The assumption is that some difficulties can be addressed adequately in as few as one to three sessions. Managed care incorporates a system of checks and balances designed to ensure

---

[1]Often these physicians are enlisted to provide care to a group of employees at a set monthly amount per person (or *per capita,* hence the trade term, "capitated care"). The fee does not fluctuate based upon the number of patients who come into the office or need the service of specialists.

continuing access to care only if the company agrees with your therapist that such care is necessary *and* fits within the scope of your benefit plan.

Two basic ingredients typical of most managed care models are designed to insure that you are getting the best necessary treatment within the limitations of the plan: *utilization review* and *case management*. Both of these mechanisms require your therapist (aka "provider") to get permission or "preauthorization" from a representative of the health plan before providing certain diagnostic or therapeutic interventions. The intent is not to delay care, but to monitor the cost, necessity and quality of your care. Unfortunately, this also means more paperwork and telephone time for your therapist outside of your sessions.

...you may have to be an active partner in the pursuit of the assistance you need... it can be empowering to accept responsibility as an active participant in your own care.

Privacy and confidentiality — traditional cornerstones of the therapeutic relationship — are a bit shaky in the new managed care environment. (There are also legal limits to confidentiality. See Appendix A for a typical therapist's confidentiality statement.) If you elect to have your health care plan pay for your brief (or other) psychotherapy, the plan's representative may become, in effect, a "third party" in the therapist's office. In other words, confidentiality in the traditional sense — your right to privacy — may be compromised if your insurance company is to pay. These days, insurance companies and other payors often require fairly detailed information about therapy clients and their treatment in order to determine whether or not to authorize additional sessions. This is in response to the need to monitor costs, yet it also is a practice many therapists *strongly* oppose. Please feel free to talk to your therapist about this issue so you can be assured regarding the degree of confidentiality.

Whether you're trying to get a first appointment authorized or your therapist has requested additional visits, you may have to be an active partner in the pursuit of the assistance you need by talking directly with your health plan's representative.

While the red tape can be frustrating, it can be empowering to accept responsibility as an active participant in your own care. Just as your brief treatment will be focused and quite specific, so will the steps required of you to obtain treatment on your behalf within a managed care benefit. Taking the time to understand these steps as a knowledgeable and educated consumer *before* you actually need help or assistance will maximize the possibility of a relatively straightforward, uncomplicated process at a time of need — when a minimum of stress may be crucial.

How Can You Tell if You're Getting Good Care?

There are some standards which may be applied to any health care situation to help you determine if you're getting quality care. Most managed care agencies use some or all of the following criteria to balance the "cost-effectiveness" equation:

- Informed consent of the patient, with ample information provided at the outset.
- Assurance of confidentiality (see Appendix A).
- Careful assessment and treatment planning.
- Objective evaluation procedures (e.g., tests, surveys, peer review by other professionals).
- Research support for treatment procedures (literature references should be available if you ask).

Putting It All Together

Now let's take a look at a few examples of folks accessing their managed mental health benefits:

George *is 27-year-old whose wife has just left him. He has never been married before, nor seen or even considered seeing a counselor. He comes from a fairly conservative background and thought only "crazy" people see shrinks, but has never been this* upset before either. He is having a hard time at work, his mind wanders, he is having difficulty sleeping and always feels tired. He doesn't know whom to talk with or even if he wants to talk. He decides that if only he could get some rest things would be better so he decides to see his doctor. His physician examines him and refers him to a counselor; he feels even more upset, as he had just wanted something to help him sleep. As he leaves the office, the nurse asks him what kind of insurance he has. He gives her his insurance card and she hands him a referral slip (or "preauthorization") for three visits. His insurance works with a "preferred provider panel" so he can look in his "participating provider book" and contact any conveniently located counselor listed. She reminds him that it is important when calling to tell the counselor not only the doctor who referred him, but the kind of insurance he has. He thinks about it, has another difficult evening and reluctantly calls the next day and gets an appointment for later in the week. By the second visit he knows he made the right decision. While he is still struggling, he has found talking helpful. The homework his therapist assigned has been useful he and feels better simply doing something to take charge of his life. Toward the end of the visit, both George and the therapist decide that it would be helpful if their work could continue so the therapist requests preauthorization for several additional visits, reminding him to work hard between sessions, as time is short and "every session counts."

Alicia is a 19-year-old sophomore at State University. An average student, her attention has recently been focused on her boyfriend, Akim. She arrived at the university psychological clinic after referral by her dorm counselor when she began talking about suicide. Akim left school, joined the Army, and told Alicia to "start dating other guys." She was devastated, and says her life is over. The sensitive receptionist at the clinic connected Alicia immediately with the "intake counselor," who did an initial assessment of her condition and of the likelihood that she would *carry through on her threat. The counselor spent nearly two hours with Alicia, then walked her to the campus physician's office for a physical evaluation and possible anti-depressant medication. Alicia signed a short "contract" with the counselor, promising that she would not make any further attempts on her life at least until she visited the counselor again two days hence. The counselor consulted with the director of the clinic and with the referral physician and developed a preliminary treatment plan for Alicia, involving three more sessions, another visit with the physician, a follow-up with the dorm counselor, and a short battery of psychological tests. After this short-term plan, Alicia will be re-evaluated to determine her need for continuing therapy at the clinic or in an outside treatment center. (State University's counseling policy allows only eight visits before referral to an outside agency.)*

Chuck *is eleven years old, has always been a good kid but has been having a hard time recently . For the last several years he has had increasing difficulty staying still in class or paying attention. He has been increasingly impulsive and impatient at home and his parents, with the teacher's support, take him to see his pediatrician at Kaiser. After hearing the history, the doctor refers them to the Department of Psychiatry for an evaluation. They see Dr. Smith, a child psychologist, who has Chuck's parents and teacher fill out a long questionnaire. Dr. Smith reviews the records and family history, interviews the family and Chuck, and administers several psychological tests. She then refers Chuck to a child psychiatrist for a medication consultation. The decision is made to see if Chuck would benefit from a trial on medication, and the family continues to talk with Dr. Smith, who assigns a number of "homework assignments" to the family in their weekly meetings. Six weeks later Chuck's parents and teacher report that he is doing much better and Dr. Smith refers Chuck back to his pediatrician, rescheduling the family for a routine follow-up appointment in three months.*

Taking Charge of Your Own Care

Basically, that's it. If you remember that *every session counts* and work hard to make the most of every one, many difficulties can improve in a short time. Don't forget that every managed care plan will have its own unique way of doing things but, in general, to access your mental health benefits you will need to:

- See what kind of mental health care your particular plan offers by reading the benefits book *entirely* and contacting your health care representative to have any questions or concerns answered, as well as verifying your understanding as a consumer and patient. Find out if you need a physician referral to see a therapist.

- Make an appointment with your primary care physician and let him or her know you need emotional support and ask that rather than simply prescribing medication for you that s/he facilitate a referral to a mental health specialist.

- Set up an appointment with the department, group or individual to which you have been referred.

- Work hard with your therapist, remembering that *every session counts*. Identify the problem(s) troubling you and work in collaboration with your therapist to determine the best course of action available to you. Follow through assertively!

- Remember both you and your therapist have responsibility for your care. Each of you needs to work actively at verifying compliance with the managed care plan's guidelines if you want them to help pay for treatment.

Afterword

Life holds the promise of joy, the hope for meaningful relationships, and opportunities to contribute to others and the community at large. But life can also be very hard, and sometimes tragic. Each person is doing her or his best to make it — to survive and to live the best life possible. Sometimes our attempts to cope are successful, but at other times the challenges are simply overwhelming. To be knocked over by life stresses is no crime or sin, but it's no picnic either. No human being is immune to feeling overwhelmed.

Psychotherapy is a valuable resource for dealing with those stresses, and brief therapy has made it possible for more and more people to benefit from that resource. Brief therapy does not attempt to "cure" people, but it does facilitate effective coping and enhances our inherent capacities for emotional healing.

You've heard us say over and over that "every session counts." Let us close by saying "your life counts." When times are hard, you owe it to yourself to take constructive action that will help you make it. You may just find the most valuable action will be your decision to pursue brief therapy.

We hope this book has been helpful, and we wish you well.

—J.P., N.V., D.L.

Appendix A. Sample Therapist's Statement on Confidentiality

The rights and welfare of those who seek psychological services are protected by state law and the professional code of ethics to which I subscribe.

Essentially, this means that information about clients revealed in the course of psychotherapy or evaluation remains strictly confidential. That is, I will need a signed release of information prior to releasing information regarding you.

You should be aware, however, that the protection of confidentiality is not absolute. There are a few specific occasions, which arise quite rarely, when a therapist may be legally or ethically compelled to release information to another. For example, if it were the therapist's judgement that the client posed an imminent danger to himself/herself or to others, the therapist might need to notify the authorities, relatives or an intended victim. In other instances a court would be entitled to client information if:

a) the court ordered and paid for the examination/evaluation, or

b) the client claimed in a legal action that his/her therapy was relevant to the outcome of that legal action.

Also, therapists are required by law to report any suspected child abuse or sexual molestation to Child Protective Services or elder abuse to Adult Protection Services. Finally, the therapist cannot promise *absolute* confidentiality to a child or adolescent client supported by and living with his parents (unemancipated minor) in regard to matters of overriding importance to his/her welfare. For example, if a child was a danger to himself/herself or others, the therapist could not hold this information confidential.

In any case, it is highly unlikely that any of these unusual situations would arise. If they should, please be assured that I will discuss the matter with you and will seek your full participation in any decisions that may be required. I will exercise both sensitivity and professional judgement in releasing only the minimal amount of information required by the particular situation.

Appendix B. Self-Rating Checklist

One potentially valuable and useful technique for more accurately measuring how you are feeling is the use of "Self-Rating Scales" like the one below. The items included are common difficulties many people experience, but not all will apply. Because we are each unique, you will find several "blanks" for you to fill in about uncomfortable areas you may want to focus on. This is a great technique to use at least once a week while in difficult times and will help you note changes and provide a more realistic perspective on how you are doing at any point in time.

Self-Rating Scale

Check only one answer to each question

0=Not at all   1=A little   2=Somewhat   3=Quite a bit   4=A lot

During the past week, how much did you suffer from:

1. Difficulty catching your breath or getting a lump
   in your throat   0 1 2 3 4
2. Chest pain, pressure or feeling as though your heart
   may be racing   0 1 2 3 4
3. Excessive sweating for no reason, feeling lightheaded
   and/or dizzy   0 1 2 3 4
4. Feeling off balance or like your legs may not
   hold you up and you could fall   0 1 2 3 4
5. Nausea or stomach problems   0 1 2 3 4
6. Feeling detached or disconnected from yourself
   and/or others   0 1 2 3 4
7. Hot or cold flashes   0 1 2 3 4
8. Feeling as though you are dying or that something
   terrible could happen at any second   0 1 2 3 4
9. Believing you are or about to "lose it"   0 1 2 3 4

10. Worrying excessively about dirt, germs or chemicals   0 1 2 3 4

11. Worrying that something bad will happen because you forgot something important like locking the door or turning something off   0 1 2 3 4

12. Unable to stop worrying that you will lose something that is really important to you   0 1 2 3 4

13. Washing or wanting to wash yourself or things around you   0 1 2 3 4

14. Checking or wanting to check things over and over or repeat them to be sure   0 1 2 3 4

15. Avoiding or wanting to avoid situations or people   0 1 2 3 4

16. Finding yourself thinking about something over and over and over again   0 1 2 3 4

17. Feeling isolated or alone   0 1 2 3 4

18. Feeling increasingly sad, blue or depressed   0 1 2 3 4

19. Having little and/or no appetite or eating just because you know you should   0 1 2 3 4

20. Having difficulty enjoying things you normally do   0 1 2 3 4

21. Being increasingly forgetful and/or having difficulty concentrating   0 1 2 3 4

22. Sleeping more or less than you normally do and/or waking up tired   0 1 2 3 4

23. Thoughts of wanting to hurt yourself or wishing you were dead   0 1 2 3 4

24. Having upsetting recollections of a traumatic event   0 1 2 3 4

25. Having recurrent dreams of a traumatic event and/or feeling as though it might be happening again   0 1 2 3 4

26. Feeling irritable and easily frustrated   0 1 2 3 4

_____   0 1 2 3 4

_____   0 1 2 3 4

_____   0 1 2 3 4

_____   0 1 2 3 4

_____   0 1 2 3 4

APPENDIX C.
Group Programs for Help with
Emotional Problems

In your efforts to deal with the emotional issues in your life — on your own and as a part of your brief therapy — you may find it helpful to consider participation in some form of group work. In most communities, there is a wide variety of therapy, self-help and support groups available to assist with emotional problems. Such groups vary tremendously: some can be very helpful; others can *create* serious emotional problems for those seeking help.

For help in locating resources in your community, contact your local Mental Health Association. Check directory information or contact: The National Mental Health Association, 1021 Prince Street, Alexandria, VA 22314-297, Phone (703) 684-7722.

Psychotherapy groups typically are led by a professional, licensed psychotherapist with specific training in group processes, psychotherapy and group dynamics. Clients enter these groups on referral from a professional, usually as an integral part of on-going therapy. Participation in such groups may last from a few weeks to a year or more, depending upon the problem focus and the needs of the clients. Some groups are highly structured toward specific behavioral changes, others involve sharing of deep personal experiences and feelings; some deal with important current stressors, others with long-standing emotional and personality difficulties. With a good therapist, group treatment is powerful and can be very helpful.

Support groups abound. Many of these are either leaderless or are led by a non-professional and are often topical: bereavement, divorce, women's or men's issues. Such groups can provide considerable support and human connection for the members. Such groups should avoid in-depth exploration of emotional concerns; there is an inherent risk of psychiatric disasters should extremely intense issues emerge in a group with an untrained leader. Caution is advised (see "Benefits and Risks" below). Self-help groups can be valuable, but if you think you need *professional* help, get it.

Organized self-help/recovery programs are often based on an established set of values, philosophies and guidelines, such as the various twelve-step programs: Alcoholics Anonymous and its dozens of clones for gambling, obesity, "co-dependency," "sexual addiction,".... Many professionals refer clients to these groups for specific needs. They can be very valuable, but here too, caution is advised (see "Benefits and Risks" below).

Potential Benefits of Self-Help Group Programs

- Validation of your feelings.
- Emotional support.
- Advice.
- Guest speakers.
- Networking.
- Affordability.
- Feedback.
- Step-by-step strategies.

Potential Risks of Self-Help Group Programs

- Intense emotional openness.
- Re-creation of maladaptive patterns.
- Charismatic or "cult" dependency.
- "One-size-fits-all."
- No screening of members.
- Unrealistic promises.
- Religious/spiritual focus you don't agree with.
- Avoiding seeking professional treatment.
- Long-term dependence on the group.
- Promise of quick cures.

Check out a group thoroughly before you join. Get references and recommendations just as you might as you try to locate a physician, dentist or therapist. Talk to the group leader and a group member prior to your first meeting. And if you do decide to attend a group, consider the first meeting as a trial visit — check it out and see if it feels right for you. *Ask questions!*

References

Alberti, R., and Emmons, M. (1995). *Your Perfect Right* (seventh edition). San Luis Obispo, CA: Impact Publishers, Inc.

Benson, H. (1975). *The Relaxation Response.* New York: Avon.

Bower, S. A. and Bower, G. H. (1994). *Asserting Your Self* (second edition). Reading, MA: Addison-Wesley Publishing Co.

Bradshaw, J. (1989). *The Family.* Deerfield Beach, FL: Health Communications, Inc.

Budman, S. and Gurman, A. (1988). *Theory and Practice of Brief Therapy.* New York: Guilford Publications, Inc.

Burns, D. D. (1980). *Feeling Good.* New York: Signet.

Davis, M., Eshelman, E. R., and McKay, M. (1995). *The Relaxation and Stress Reduction Workbook* (fourth edition). Oakland, CA: New Harbinger.

Lerner, H. G. (1989). *The Dance of Intimacy.* New York: Harper and Row.

Peck, M. S. (1978). *The Road Less Traveled.* New York: Simon and Schuster, Inc.

Preston, J. (1993). *Growing Beyond Emotional Pain: Action Plans for Healing.* San Luis Obispo, CA: Impact Publishers, Inc.

Rakos, R. F. and Schroeder, H. E. (1980). *Self-Directed Assertiveness Training* (audiotape). New York: Guilford Publications, Inc.

Strupp, H. (1969). "Lessons that Patients Learn in Psychotherapy," *Archives of General Psychiatry,* Vol. 21. Pages 203-212.

Regarding Medication Treatment

- General Reference: Preston, J. and Johnson, J. (1995). *Clinical Psychopharmacology: Made Ridiculously Simple* (Second Edition). MedMaster Inc.
- Depression: Preston, J. (1989). *You Can Beat Depression: A Guide To Recovery.* San Luis Obispo, CA: Impact Publishers, Inc.
- Anxiety: Sheehan, D. (1983). *The Anxiety Disease.* New York: Bantam Books
- Bi-Polar: Fieve, R. (1989) *Moodswings.* New York: Bantam Books
- Psychosis: Torrey, E.F. (1988) *Surviving Schizophrenia: A Family Manual.* New York: Harper and Row.
- Obsessive-Compulsive Disorder: Rapoport, J. (1989) *The Boy Who Couldn't Stop Washing.* New York: Dutton .

Index

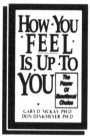

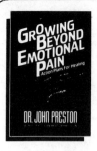